The Princeton Review

Cracking the
PRAXIS II: NTE

Cracking the
PRAXIS II: NTE

BY CORNELIA COCKE

2ND EDITION

RANDOM HOUSE, INC.
NEW YORK 1997

www.PrincetonReview.com

Princeton Review Publishing, L.L.C.
2315 Broadway
New York, NY 10024
E-mail: booksupport@review.com

ISBN 0-679-78396-2
ISSN 1090-0136

Editor: Amy Zavatto
Production Editor: Amy Bryant
Designer: Illeny Maaza

Manufactured in the United States of America.

9 8 7

2nd Edition

ACKNOWLEDGMENTS

I'd like to thank Jeannie Yoon, Amy Zavatto, P.J. Waters, Amy Bryant, Chris Kensler, John Katzman, and Chris Baumer for their sunny optimism and invaluable help.

CONTENTS

Acknowledgments   v

PART I: OVERVIEW   1

1   **Orientation**   3
2   **How to Think About the Praxis II: NTE**   7

PART II: HOW TO CRACK THE PRAXIS II: NTE   11

3   **Cracking the System: Basic Principles**   13
4   **Advanced Principles**   19
5   **What to Do on Test Day**   25

PART III: HOW TO CRACK THE TEST OF GENERAL KNOWLEDGE   29

6   **Social Studies**   31
7   **Math**   39
8   **Literature and Fine Arts**   55
9   **Science**   63

PART IV: HOW TO CRACK THE TEST OF COMMUNICATION SKILLS   71

10   **Listening**   73
11   **Reading**   77
12   **Writing**   85
13   **The Essay**   105

PART V: HOW TO CRACK THE TEST OF PROFESSIONAL KNOWLEDGE 109

14 **Professional Knowledge** 111

PART VI: THE PRINCETON REVIEW DIAGNOSTIC TEST 119

Praxis II: NTE Diagnostic Answer Key 222

About the Author 224

PART I

Overview

1

Orientation

WHAT IS THE NTE?

The NTE Core Battery is just one part of the huge Praxis Series, a group of standardized tests designed to measure the skills and knowledge of beginning teachers. In order to be certified to teach in some states, you must earn a passing score on various tests in the Praxis Series. Passing scores vary from state to state.

Obviously, before signing up for anything, check the requirements for your state.

WHAT'S ON THE NTE?

The NTE Core Battery is really three separate tests, each composed of four 30-minute sections. Here's what each test covers:

Test of General Knowledge

Social Studies	(30 questions)
Math	(25 questions)
Literature and Fine Arts	(35 questions)
Science	(30 questions)

Test of Communication Skills

Listening	(40 questions)
Reading	(30 questions)
Writing	(45 questions)
Essay	

Test of Professional Knowledge

4 sections*	(35 questions each)

Seems kind of daunting, doesn't it? It's not as bad as it looks. For some sections (Literature and Fine Arts, Social Studies, and Science) you need to have only basic knowledge about the particular subject. And we mean *basic*. It's not college-level. All you will need is just a bit of review.

For other sections (Math and Writing) you need some fundamental skills, but they can be learned in a relatively short amount of time by using this book. The Test of Professional Knowledge requires common sense more than anything else; any education classes you've taken will be a big help.

WHAT'S UP WITH THE NTE?

You should take the tests separately, on different days. You'll definitely get a higher score if you don't take all three tests on the same day. (Although that's what most people do, because they just want to get it over with.)

How Is the NTE Scored?

You'll get a separate score for each test, roughly from 600 to 695. The actual scoring of the tests is extremely complicated. For the Test of General Knowledge, the total number of correct answers in each section is multiplied by a "weighting factor" to arrive at the raw score for that section. All four raw scores are added together and converted into the scaled score. The Test of Communication Skills is scored the same way, with the exception of the Essay (scoring for that is discussed in chapter 13). For the Test of Professional Knowledge, the total number of correct answers on all three sections is added and converted to a scaled score without multiplying by a "weighting factor." (The conversion chart changes somewhat from test to test; that's how ETS attempts to adjust for some tests being harder than others. So the same raw score won't necessarily convert to the same scaled score on different test administrations.)

Does any of that matter to you? Only a little. The two really important things you need to know are:

- You won't be penalized for wrong answers the way you were on the SAT and on many other standardized tests.

- You can afford to miss a lot of questions and still earn a passing score.

Both of these points will be discussed in more detail in later chapters.

Where Does the NTE Come from?

It's brought to you compliments of the Educational Testing Service (ETS), a tax-exempt private company that's responsible for a zillion standardized tests ranging from the SAT to those for barbers and CIA agents.

How Is the NTE Different from the SAT?

It's longer, for one thing. Painfully longer. Which means that stamina is very important. You've got to be able to stay focused even after many hours of sitting in an uncomfortable chair filling in bubbles for your answers. We can't quantify it, but we're willing to bet the farm that a lot of people do poorly on the NTE simply because they get tired and start making bubbling errors, or just can't concentrate well enough to get the answers right. (We understand. After eight hours or so, it's hard to care anymore.)

Another big difference, as we've already pointed out, is that the NTE (Test of General Knowledge) sometimes asks questions that require you to know specific facts, such as *What is John Marshall known for?* or *What is the function of fibrovascular bundles?* This specificity means that if you have a real weakness in one of the subject areas, you should do some review, at least to familiarize yourself with basic terminology.

Internet Assistance

To find out when and where to take the NTE, and whether your state requires it, you can check out the Praxis Web page at http://etsis1.ets.org/praxis/

How Can The Princeton Review Help?

The Princeton Review has been coaching standardized test takers since 1981. We understand how the tests work, and we know the most efficient ways to beat them. If you've never liked standardized tests before, we want that to change. We'll explain the attitude of a good test taker, how to use process of elimination effectively, the way to approach particular question types, and how to guess. If you follow our advice, taking the NTE won't be nearly as bad as you expect it to be.

One Last Thing . . .

The best way to study for the NTE is to focus only on the material you'll be tested on and to use only questions like the ones you'll see on the NTE. For that reason, run right out and get yourself a copy of *A Guide to the NTE Core Battery Tests*, published by ETS (or write or call ETS and order a copy). This official guide is the only published copy of an actual test, and it's an invaluable tool both for measuring how well you'll do and for practicing on real questions.

We suggest reading *Cracking the NTE* first, so you can review the subject areas and learn our techniques. Then, use our diagnostic test to practice, and, after that, move on to the official guide.

2

How to Think About the Praxis II: NTE

TEACHER, TEACHER, I DECLARE . . .

We've spent a lot of time in classrooms over the years, both as teachers and as students. Of course, the first requirement of a good teacher is that he know the material—but what separates good teachers from bad ones, or even so-so ones, is that they can hold their students' attention and make their students want to listen and perform well.

And how does the NTE Core Battery measure that? It doesn't. The NTE exists only so that state governments can say that they're doing something to maintain standards in the classroom. It doesn't really measure your knowledge of the subject either, because the stress and artificiality of the test can lead to lower scores than you deserve.

ARE YOU A GENIUS OR AN IDIOT?

It's true that some questions in General Knowledge and Professional Knowledge are fact-based, but it's important to know that we are not talking college-level questions here. Success on the NTE depends much more on your ability to handle multiple-choice questions in a test-taking situation than anything else. So if you've been thinking all these years that your standardized test scores are an accurate measure of your intelligence, knowledge, or fitness as a human being, forget it. They are simply nothing more than a measure of your ability to take standardized tests.

BUT I'VE NEVER BEEN GOOD AT STANDARDIZED TESTS

That's what a lot of people say—including people who have distinguished themselves in their course work, earning GPAs to die for. It doesn't surprise us that a person who is a great student can be a bad test taker, because the two skills have very little in common. Take a look at this chart showing the skills most rewarded in school and on your standardized test:

School	NTE
critical thinking	slavish obedience to directions
contemplation	speed
persistence	willingness to skip anything difficult
creativity	blind acceptance of the questions and answer choices

Now clearly, the school skills make for a better employee, and probably a better person. But these two sets of skills don't have to be mutually exclusive—you can be a good student and a good test taker as long as you alter your usual behavior while practicing for and taking the NTE.

But the Whole Thing Makes Me Break into a Rash

That's the good student talking. Good students expect to know the answers when they take tests. Which isn't surprising—they've taken good notes, listened in class, done the reading, and studied. So they aren't used to sitting down on test day and seeing questions they have no idea how to answer.

But that happens to everybody on standardized tests, and the NTE is no exception.

Okay, So What Does a Good Test Taker Do Then?

On a tough question, a good test taker shrugs, guesses, and moves on. To use a baseball analogy, you have to have the mind-set of a star hitter: Even the greatest baseball players can't get a hit more than once every three times at bat. That's a lot of strikes, a lot of whiffs, a lot of failure. What makes those great players great is that after they get a strike, they forget about it—the next time they come to the plate they are totally focused on that pitch, and that pitch only. They expect to hit it out of the park instead of being upset about how they screwed up before.

Drastic Measures

The NTE measures how well you take the NTE—not your brains, academic aptitude, or teaching skill.

What Does That Have to Do with Me?

Let's say you're asked the following question:

What is Henry Clay known for?

And let's say you don't know Henry Clay from a hole in the ground. If you're a good test taker, you chuckle to yourself, guess, and move on without wasting more than two or three seconds. And when you read the next question, you've forgotten all about Henry Clay. Just like Ken Griffey Jr. or Ted Williams, you're only focused on the present moment, not on past failures.

But Can I Really Afford to Blow a Lot of Questions?

You bet, baby. You can miss approximately 50 General Knowledge questions and still pass—that's more than 12 questions per section! You can miss approximately 18 Communications questions, or about 9 questions per section. And you can miss approximately 30 Professional Knowledge questions, a little more than 7 per section. (The numbers are approximate because the conversion tables change from test to test.)

Of course, this doesn't mean that the most work you'll have to do is keep your no. 2 pencil sharp—but it does mean you have room to breathe. For example, if you know a lot about art and literature but almost nothing about science, you can still do fine as long as you make sure you get those art and literature questions right.

Here are the passing sores for each of the tests in 1996 (based on a 600–695 scale):

	General Knowledge	Communication Skills	Professional Knowledge
Arizona			642
CAE*	656	659	
ODDS**		655	
Hawaii	647	651	648
Kansas			642
Kentucky	643	646	644
Indiana	647	653	646
Louisiana	644	645	645
Maine	649	656	648
Maryland	645	648	648
Mississippi	646	651	649
Missouri			638
Montana	644	648	648
Nevada			651
New Jersey	649		
New Mexico	645	644	630
New York	649	650	646
North Carolina			649
Ohio	642		
Pennsylvania	644	646	
Rhode Island	649	657	
Tennessee	647	651	
Virginia	639	649	

* Council for Academic Excellence (Ohio)

** Department of Defense Dependent Schools

The median score ranges are roughly 650–665 for General Knowledge, 654–668 for Communication Skills, and 655–669 for Professional Knowledge. That's where the middle 50 percent of test takers are scoring—which is well *above* a passing score in almost every state.

How Low Can You Go?

Two states with some of the lowest passing scores are Louisiana and New Mexico (and New Orleans and Santa Fe are very cool places to live).

PART ◆ II

How to Crack the
Praxis II: NTE

3

Cracking the System: Basic Principles

If you hate standardized tests, you've probably been approaching them the wrong way, as we explained in chapter 2. In chapters 3 and 4, we'll explain some important—crucially important—principles and techniques for handling the NTE. If you follow these techniques religiously, your score will go up, guaranteed.

PRINCIPLE #1: GUESS!

Principle Quiz #1

Why should you *never* leave a question blank on your answer sheet?

You won't be penalized for wrong answers, so *don't leave anything blank*. Not having a guessing penalty is the best thing that can happen to you, because it means you don't risk anything by guessing—even when you haven't read the question. It also means that pacing is much easier.

Here's why: Let's say you don't have time to get to the last ten questions in a section, and you simply bubble in (B) for each of those ten questions. There's a good chance that the right answer to two of those ten questions will be (B). You'll earn two points even without having read the questions. (If there are five answer choices, you have a one in five chance of guessing it right; if there are four answer choices, your odds are one in four, even better.)

When you finish a section, check your answer sheet to make sure you've bubbled in an answer for every single question.

AND THAT'S NOT ALL . . .

By far the biggest reason people lose points on standardized tests is that they go too fast, making careless mistakes on questions they could have gotten right. Since you'll still earn some points from guessing, you can afford to slow down. Do each question thoroughly, avoiding careless mistakes like the plague. On some sections you'll want to guess on a pretty large number of questions so you'll have plenty of time to work on those you know and can get right. And by "guess," we don't mean read it, think about it, work on it, and then guess—we mean guess blindly, bubbling in whichever letter you've chosen beforehand as your lucky letter.

Answer to Principle Quiz #1

Because you won't be penalized for a wrong answer.

HOW DOES THAT WORK, EXACTLY?

Choose a letter—A, B, C, D—and bubble in that letter *every time* you don't get to a question or decide to "skip" a question. (The only thing you "skip" is doing the work, not the space on your answer sheet.) The advantage of choosing one letter ahead of time is that you won't have to think about it on test day, and you statistically increase your chances slightly by using the same letter over and over.

What about answer choice E? Well, in the Listening Section there are only four choices, so there is no E. It's a good idea to simplify matters and pick a letter that will be valid for all the sections.

WAIT A MINUTE—SHOULDN'T I TRY TO GET ALL THE ANSWERS RIGHT?

No. You aren't going to get them all right no matter how hard you try, because standardized tests aren't designed that way. You'll get a much higher score if you try to get every question *you spend time on* right and then just guess on the leftovers. The way to get a higher score on a standardized test is to avoid making careless errors and to guess intelligently when you get stuck. (More on that in chapter 4, Advanced Principles.)

SPECIAL NOTE TO WOMEN

Men do better on standardized tests than women do. Shocking, isn't it? Think of this as more proof that these tests can't be measuring intelligence or knowledge but rather certain limited skills, such as the willingness to take risks and the ability to follow directions. Generally speaking, men feel more comfortable guessing than women do. In our experience—having taught thousands of students over the years—more women want to *know* their answer is right before bubbling it in, whereas more guys will happily guess on questions they've never looked at, hoping to strike it rich.

As we've explained, guessing will definitely raise your score. So if you're naturally on the cautious side, you'll have to force yourself to guess, at least at first. Keep in mind that our guessing technique does not mean that you will guess correctly all the time or even most of the time. Some of your guesses will be right, and some will be wrong. And that will get you a higher score.

> **Principle Quiz #2**
> What's the best way to get the right answer to an NTE question?

PRINCIPLE #2: USE PROCESS OF ELIMINATION

Learning how to use Process of Elimination (POE from now on) is the most important technique you'll get from this book. It sounds easy enough, and you may think you already use it. But *really* using POE takes practice and discipline. Why? Because all through your years at school, you've been trained to focus on the right answers. To use POE effectively, you must focus on the *wrong* answers, so you can eliminate them.

WHAT'S SO HARD ABOUT THAT?

Nothing, really—it's just a matter of changing your perspective and practicing the technique. Taking a standardized test is frustrating. You have no control over the answers. You can't write your own answer in the margin, phrasing it exactly as you'd like. You are stuck with what they give you. And the right answer may not look quite the way you want it to—in fact, it may strike you as too simplistic, too obvious, incomplete, or just plain blah. It may be all of those things, and it's possible you could have written a much better answer yourself but it's a waste of time to worry about that, because you can't change the test.

> **Answer to Principle Quiz #2**
> Eliminate the rest of the answer choices

You can change the way you take the test, though. So understand that what makes that answer right is that there is nothing explicitly wrong with it. In other words, it doesn't have to be a good answer, it just has to be better than the other three or four.

Your job is to scrutinize those answer choices, find their flaws, and cross them out until only one answer remains. Don't do this in your head. When we say *cross it out* we mean literally take your pencil and draw a line through the letter of that answer. Unless you eliminate all four wrong answers on your first pass, you're going to have to go back through them; it's much easier if you know exactly which answers are still in the running. Avoid relying on your memory for anything on the NTE, no matter how small or insignificant the task may seem.

WHY ISN'T THE RIGHT ANSWER MORE RIGHT?

It's just the nature of standardized tests. If the test writers made the right answer perfect, it would be hard to miss—and too many people would get high scores. If too many people get high scores, then a high score doesn't mean anything, and the test would be useless. For a standardized test to be considered useful, test takers have to score over a broad range, with the majority scoring somewhere around the middle. To make sure that happens, the test writers make the right answer look a bit less appealing—and they stick in a few wrong answers that look pretty good if you aren't really paying attention.

WHAT IF I DISAGREE WITH THEIR ANSWER?

Don't go there. Approach the NTE on its own terms, and don't argue with it. It's good to be aggressive, but direct your aggression in a way that will raise your score. ETS will be able to explain the right answers to all of the questions on the NTE by pointing out the flaws in the other four choices. So you want to take the same approach. Rather than justifying your answer as the correct one, be ready to explain why you eliminated the rest.

PRINCIPLE #3: DON'T RUSH

Rushing leads directly to careless mistakes. Experiment to find the right pace—as fast as you can manage without missing questions you should have gotten right. You shouldn't spend time on every question in every section. If you do, you'll very likely lower your score. Analyze your practice sections carefully. If you made more than one or two careless mistakes, you were going too fast. If you didn't make any careless mistakes, try to go a little faster next time.

BUT I NEVER, EVER FINISH A SECTION...

The inverse of Principle #3 is *don't dawdle*. Some test takers want to be so absolutely certain of their answer that they double-check it, triple-check it, and second-guess it, making themselves crazy in the process. Do you worry and

Principle Quiz #3

What's the best way to pace yourself during a section?

(A) allow a specific time limit for each question
(B) do the section really fast to save time for checking your work
(C) work through the questions in a painstaking manner, triple-checking as you go along
(D) none of the above

Answer to Principle Quiz #3

(D) none of the above. (A) is unrealistic and just adds pressure, and (B) and (C) are too extreme. If you find yourself missing questions that you really know, you're going too fast. If you make very few errors but don't get to a lot of questions, you're going too slow.

worry over an answer, only to find out your first instinct was right? Then hurry yourself along. Do you allow yourself to get fixated on a particular question, thinking that you can't move on until you solve it? Break yourself of that habit now. No single question is worth any more points than any other. If you get stuck on something, blow it off and keep going.

PRINCIPLE #4: ONE TEST AT A TIME

Yeah, yeah, we know: You just want to get it over with. Or you have scheduling problems. Whatever. You know in your heart we're right. If you are the least bit worried about passing any of the three tests in the Core Battery, you should not take all three at once. Most people do, and it hurts their scores.

   If you take them separately, you gain two big advantages: Fatigue is hardly an issue, since you'll take four sections instead of twelve; and you can study much more thoroughly for the test at hand. If you take the whole thing at once you have *nine* different section types to study for—why put yourself through that?

SUMMARY

1. Don't leave anything blank on your answer sheet. For all questions you don't have time for, bubble in the letter you've chosen in advance. If you get stuck after eliminating even one choice, guess from the remaining choices. At the end of the section, check your answer sheet to make sure there aren't any blank bubbles.

2. Accept the fact that you will not do every question on every section. The number of questions you should do depends on your knowledge of the material in the section and on how fast you can work without making errors. Most people should not finish either the math section or the reading section, because the questions in both of those sections take a fair amount of time to do well. We'll discuss this more thoroughly in the chapters for each of these sections.

3. Work as fast as you can without making careless mistakes. If you get a question wrong because you misread it, misbubbled it, or made a goofy computation error, you are throwing points out the window. Work carefully, and that means never giving in to the temptation to rush.

4. Don't take all three tests on the same day. Enough said.

4

Advanced Principles

Some of the following may not seem so advanced. In fact, some of the information may seem downright obvious. But successful standardized test takers adhere to these principles not just occasionally, but all the time. Practice them, learn them, live them.

PRINCIPLE #1: READ THE QUESTION CAREFULLY

A lot of mistakes are made because test takers don't follow the directions exactly. And you can waste a lot of time roaming through the answer choices feeling lost, only because you don't really know what the question asked for.

So read the question slowly. Read it again. Paraphrase it. And after you spend time reading the answer choices or doing computations, go back and read the question again before continuing.

Whenever you get stuck, the first thing to do is read the question again, and make sure you understand every word.

EXCEPT/LEAST/NOT

These are easy to miss, because you're asked to pick the wrong answer, which goes against everything you've ever done in school. When you see one of these, circle the EXCEPT or underline it; do something to make it stick in your mind. Then read your answer choices and eliminate the *right* answers.

CHARTS

These could show up on the Science, Social Studies, Math, and Professional Knowledge sections. They're not difficult, but that doesn't mean people don't blow them all the time by rushing through and not being careful enough. If the question asks about widget production in November, take your pencil and point exactly to the right product and the right month on the chart. Your eyes can get tired and confused, and it helps to have a physical way to focus your attention.

PRINCIPLE #2: USE THE THREE-PASS SYSTEM

The Three-Pass System is a method to pace yourself to get the most points possible out of every section. Instead of spending time equally on all the questions, you're going to spend the most time where it will do you the most good—that is, on the questions you have the best chance of getting right.

First Pass: Go through the entire section, doing only those questions that seem easy. If anything looks at all difficult, circle it and keep moving. You should spend the bulk of your time answering First Pass questions. They're easy, so take the time to get them right.

Second Pass: Go back and tackle the questions you kinda-sorta know. Make sure to use partial knowledge (see Principle #3 on page 21) and POE.

Third Pass: Go to your bubble sheet and fill in your pre-selected answer choice for anything you don't have an answer for. Obviously, the Third Pass should only take you a few minutes, tops.

But Shouldn't I Do the Questions in Order?

No. For most sections, the questions aren't really in any order of difficulty, because that depends largely on what you happen to know. (One exception is the Math section, on which the questions do get somewhat harder as you go along.) Keep in mind that you don't get any more points for getting a difficult question right, so it makes sense to spend more time on the easier questions and to do them first.

On every section except Listening, you can answer the questions in whatever order you like; it's one of the things you have some control over. So, if on first glance a question seems hard, skip it. Don't feel like a failure because a question is hard or asks about something you've never heard of. Remember, you aren't supposed to get them all right. If you're having a bad moment and get stuck, circle the question number and come back for it on the Second Pass. A troublesome question often seems easy when you see it the second time.

One last thing—all this skipping around can cause bubbling mayhem unless you're quite careful. Just follow the directions in Principle #6 (see page 22).

PRINCIPLE #3: USE PARTIAL KNOWLEDGE

On some fact-based questions you may know more than you think you do—and that may be plenty to get the correct answer.

Let's go back to our example from chapter 2, and this time we'll give you some answer choices.

What is Henry Clay known for?

(A) He was the instigator of the Boston Tea Party.

(B) Along with Thomas Jefferson, he negotiated the Louisiana Purchase, which doubled the territory of the United States.

(C) As a member of the Continental Congress, he denounced British rule in his "Give me liberty or give me death" speech.

(D) He authored the Compromise of 1850, which attempted to placate both free and slave-holding states in order to avert civil war.

(E) He developed the first system of mass production in America, making automobiles affordable for the general public.

All righty then. Remember that you don't have to know who Henry Clay was, you just have to try to eliminate some answers. What time period is he from? If you vaguely know that he had something to do with the Civil War, eliminate all non-Civil War answers. You end up with (D), the right answer.

If you couldn't place Henry Clay around the time of the Civil War, you can still eliminate some trap answers. Are there any other Henrys in the answer choices? You can eliminate (E), that's Henry Ford, the auto pioneer. And choice (C)? That's Patrick Henry.

So you may not know what Henry Clay did, but if you know he didn't sell cars, you're on your way to a right answer. Eliminating just one answer choice significantly improves your odds of getting the right answer.

PRINCIPLE #4: YOUR OPINION COUNTS FOR NOTHING

Your only goal on the NTE is to earn a passing score and go home. You do not want to argue with the test or rely on your own opinions to answer questions. Sometimes, particularly in the Professional Knowledge sections—but also in Reading, Fine Arts and Literature, Science, and Social Studies—you may see questions about topics you have opinions about. Maybe even strong opinions. It does not matter.

Stay focused on eliminating wrong answers, not on what you think about the topic at hand.

PRINCIPLE #5: TRAP ANSWERS

Trap answers look good if you're going too fast or not thinking clearly. In our Henry Clay example, the answer about Henry Ford was a trap answer—the word *Henry* starts ringing in your ears, and before you know it, you've picked the wrong answer.

Don't leap at the first thing that seems possible. Remember that you should always look at the answers skeptically and try to eliminate them.

TRUE STATEMENT, WRONG ANSWER

Sometimes you'll run across an answer choice that is true but simply not the answer to the question. You can avoid picking it if you're using POE instead of jumping at the first answer that sounds halfway decent. Also remember Principle #1—reread the question whenever you feel even the tiniest bit disconnected from it.

PRINCIPLE #6: BUBBLING

Circle your answers in your test booklet as you go along. When you finish a page, bubble them on your answer sheet. Don't bubble them in one by one, and don't wait until the end of the section to start bubbling madly. Why is this the best method?

- ◆ If you bubble in one by one, you're constantly zigzagging your attention from one paper to another. This breaks your concentration.

- If you skip around, and you should, you're much less likely to make a mistake if you bubble in groups.

- You may be working at a small desk, where you don't have room for both answer sheet and test booklet to be accessible at the same time.

- Circling answers in your test booklet makes it easy to check for and correct bubbling mistakes. Your booklet is collected by the proctor, so you'll have a record of your answers in case anything happens to your answer sheet later on.

When the proctor announces five minutes left in the section, start bubbling in one by one so you don't get caught with unbubbled answers.

SUMMARY

1. Read the question slowly and carefully. Make sure you understand exactly what it says.

2. Use the Three-Pass System. Go through the section answering the easiest questions first, then return for any questions you kind of know. In the last couple of minutes, bubble in guesses for the remainder. Be careful with your bubbling.

3. Use partial knowledge to eliminate answers. Just because you couldn't answer the question by itself doesn't mean you can't get it right using POE. A lot of time even the slightest, vaguest knowledge will be enough to earn you a point.

4. Leave your opinions at the door to the test room. Don't argue with the test writers or the questions—the only thing you should be aggressively critical about are the answer choices.

5. Avoid trap answers by not working too quickly. Be disciplined in using POE, and make sure you always know exactly what the question is asking.

6. Bubble in your answers in groups. Usually that's a page at a time; for reading passages, do them a passage at a time. In the last five minutes of each section, bubble in a question at a time.

5

What to Do on Test Day

THE WEEK BEFORE

What to study depends on your particular strengths and weaknesses. If you have a problem with math, do a ton of problems this week. Make up flash cards to review terminology for Professional Knowledge, Social Studies, and Science.

Act like you're training for the Olympics—you're about to experience a lot of stress and pressure, and the way to combat it is to take care of yourself. Eat right, get plenty of sleep, and try to study in the morning, which is when you'll probably be taking the NTE.

However, this is *not* the time to quit smoking, go on a diet, or start a major exercise program. The idea is to reduce stress, not compound it.

THE NIGHT BEFORE

Don't try to cram in a lifetime's worth of chemistry and physics now. Your short-term memory hasn't got that much room, and you'll end up making yourself nuts. If you want to do some review or practice some math problems, do it early in the day. That night, go to a movie and relax. Have a beer. Chill. Just make sure to go to bed early.

THE MORNING OF

Get up in plenty of time—we're continually hearing horror stories of people who barely got to the test center on time, ragged and sweaty before the test had even begun. Or stories of people who were locked out because they were a few minutes late. And, the earlier you get your butt out of bed, the more time you'll have for a little pre-test prep:

- If you're concerned about your math score, do some easy problems during breakfast to get warmed up.

- Read some serious articles in the paper to get the verbal part of your brain working.

- Take a quick walk so that your body is really awake.

AT THE TEST CENTER

Sometimes it's the simplest things that get overlooked. However, if you show up to the test without the proper ID, for example, you're out of luck. You won't be allowed to take the test. So, here's what you'll need:

- a picture ID

- your ticket

- plenty of sharpened no. 2 pencils with erasers

It's also good idea to take something to read (any study notes would be great). You probably won't be allowed to take any food or coffee into the testing room, so don't go in hungry.

Bob Costas Advises...

When you do practice problems, use a no.2 pencil instead of a pen, because it's better to imitate actual test conditions in every way possible.

Avoid chatting with any terror-stricken fellow test takers. You're looking to hold on to whatever inner peace you have, and you don't need to hear about anyone else's anxiety attack.

You'll quickly realize that patience is one of the skills tested on the NTE, because the preliminaries seem to go on forever. You wait in line to get in the room, wait some more for everyone to be seated, wait while the proctor reads through the directions and everyone fills out the forms, and wait for the signal to begin. Stay calm, and don't think about what you'll do if you fail, your late car payments, your ex-boyfriend, or anything else. Get ready to focus on the first question, and that's it.

During the Test

Always remember that you can flub a question or even a section and still do fine. If you lose your concentration, don't panic. Just shake it off and go on to the next question.

If you finish a section early, force yourself to go back to any questions you had doubts about (you should have circled them the first time through). Double-check your bubbles. If you still have extra time, start working through questions again, especially if you're in the math section (that's where most test takers make the most careless errors).

There's always somebody in the room madly rustling pages only twenty seconds after the section has begun. And everyone else in the room immediately thinks, *Oh no, I'm way behind, that person is really smart and I'm a total failure.* Well, don't fall for it. Either that person is going way too fast and making tons of careless errors (in which case you can feel smug) or that person is using the Three-Pass System but not finding any easy questions (in which case you can also feel smug).

After the Test

When you're finished, the proctor will tell you that you can cancel your score immediately by signing a form. Don't do it. At the end of a grueling test, you're in a weakened condition, and it's not the time to make big decisions. You'll have a week to decide, and, unless you had a total breakdown, you probably shouldn't cancel. The questions you got wrong are the ones that tend to stick in your mind afterward, and as you know, some wrong answers are to be expected.

A Month After the Test

About four weeks after the test, you'll receive a form in the mail with all the information you bubbled in on your registration and test forms. You'll also get your score, the average range for that test, and a breakdown for each section with the number of raw points you earned and the total number of raw points available.

If you passed, you can do a jig, file the form, and forget about it.

If you didn't pass, the information on the form is quite helpful—you'll be able to see exactly which sections cost you the most points, so you'll know where to focus your studies for next time.

No Laughing Matter
If you have to go to the bathroom in the middle of a section, you won't be able to make up the time lost.

PART ◆ III

How to Crack the Test of General Knowledge

6

Social Studies

BUT I HAVEN'T TAKEN SOCIAL STUDIES IN YEARS!

Not to worry. To crack the Social Studies section, you need to do three things: use Process of Elimination effectively, read charts and maps carefully, and review some basic events and terminology. Although you'll be asked some rather difficult fact-based questions, the level of knowledge you need for the bulk of the section is not very high or very detailed. A lot of the information you need to get the right answers is given to you, either in the charts and maps, or in the questions themselves.

For example, a typical question might ask you about a constitutional amendment—but you won't have to know which amendment it is. They'll give you a few lines, and you pick the answer that's the best paraphrase. That's it.

WHAT EXACTLY DOES THE SECTION COVER?

American history, almost exclusively. Most of the questions on non-American topics will involve geography, so it wouldn't be a bad idea to spend some time looking through a world atlas.

Many of the American history questions will not ask for really specific information—you won't need to remember the details of the French and Indian War, or the date of the conference in Yalta. You will have to know general information, such as what century the Civil War was fought in, when and why the atomic bomb was first dropped, and the importance of the McCarthy hearings. Remember, as we keep saying, you aren't expected to know every single answer. If you draw a blank, or you're asked about something you've never heard of, just make a good guess and keep going.

> **STATS—SOCIAL STUDIES SECTION**
>
> Number of questions: 30
>
> Percentage of fact-based questions: 65%
>
> Order of difficulty: no
>
> Question types: approximately 10 questions on maps or charts; 0–1 question on political cartoons; 8 questions on short reading passages; 10 straight questions
>
> Techniques: POE
>
> Bubbling: page by page

QUICK REVIEW

You do need some basic knowledge to ace this section, so take the following quiz and see how you stand. If you're unable to answer more than five questions, you should probably dig out your old social studies book and review it for a night or two.

QUICK QUIZ

Answer the following questions on the lines below. (Keep in mind that the NTE section will be easier, because you'll have answer choices to help you.) The answers are on page 37.

1. Who instituted the New Deal?

2. What is laissez-faire capitalism?

3. Define sociology, anthropology, and demography.

4. When was the Depression? Who was president?

5. Which president decided to drop the atomic bomb?

6. What was agrarianism?

7. Who was Sojourner Truth?

8. Define socialism and progressivism.

9. During which war did the My Lai Massacre occur?

10. What is the AFL-CIO an example of?

11. Who was Joseph McCarthy?

12. Who is Henry Kissinger?

13. Name as many rights guaranteed by the Bill of Rights as you can.

14. What is a nuclear family?

15. Define industrialization, urbanization, and imperialism.

16. What did Susan B. Anthony fight for?

17. What does SALT stand for?

18. Why was the *Brown v. Board of Education* decision important?

19. What is détente?

20. Define inflation.

Run Straight to the Nearest Bookstore

Get a copy of *Don't Know Much About History*, by Kenneth C. Davis. It's concise, fun to read, and a terrific way to fill in the gaps in your history knowledge.

CRACKING THE QUESTION TYPES

Definitions

These questions ask you to define a word or phrase or ask you to choose the best example of something, like *recession*. They're simple if you know the word and hard if you don't. Try this one:

Which of the following is most likely to be one result of a recession?

(A) Two countries sign an extradition treaty.

(B) Retail sales drop, as well as new investments.

(C) Average salaries increase, along with consumer prices.

(D) The stock market fluctuates in response to a rumor about the president's health.

(E) The average amount of a savings account is higher than it was the year before.

Here's how to crack it

If you know what a recession is, you know the answer. But what if you don't? Don't skip it or guess randomly—let's see what we can eliminate first. Have you ever heard of a recession? It's an economics word, right? Then cross out answer (A). Is a recession a good thing or a bad thing? If you think it's bad (and it is) go to the remaining answer choices. C and E are both positive results, so cross them out. Choice D is up and down. Choice B is the only negative effect, and that's the answer. (A recession is a slowing-down of economic activity.)

So you can get a right answer when you really have only a vague sense of what's going on. Don't give up when you see unfamiliar terms. Instead, use the answer choices to help you. Maybe you thought the word *recession* reminded you of *recede*, and you looked for something moving backward; that's a good way to get the right answer, too.

One last thing. If you really have *no clue* what the word or phrase means, don't let yourself get stuck on the question. Keep a decent pace. You can always circle the number in your test booklet and come back to it when you've finished the section.

MAPS AND CHARTS

Almost half the questions in the section will ask you about a map or a chart. If your visual skills are better than your verbal skills, you're in luck. Even if they're not, map and chart questions tend to be pretty easy if you don't rush them.

What's so great about a map? Well, usually all the information you need will be right there in front of you. All you have to do is take a moment to assess the map *before* you read the question. What does the map or chart cover? Is there anything confusing about it? Does it have a key explaining symbols or shading? Understand your map or chart thoroughly, and only then approach the question. Answering the question will go a lot faster and you'll be more accurate if you invest the time to understand the map first. Here's one for practice.

History Bonus Round

On what date did Thomas Jefferson—author of the Declaration of Independence—die?

The map above shows the state-by-state results of the presidential election of 1860. Which of the following candidates won the majority of the votes in the states that are shaded here?

(A) Henry Clay
(B) Jefferson Davis
(C) Abraham Lincoln
(D) Stephen Douglas
(E) John Brown

Do you *really* need to know who won the majority of votes in the shaded areas? No. To answer this question correctly, it helps to know that the Civil War happened in the 1860s. This allows us to eliminate answer choices (A) and (B) immediately. Henry Clay died before 1860, and Jefferson Davis was the president of the Confederacy, had it succeeded in seceding. Abraham Lincoln, answer choice (C), was president during the Civil War and the North supported him in his election. Looks like we have a winner here: the correct answer is (C). Stephen Douglas lost to Lincoln in the Election of 1860, and John Brown was an abolitionist who was executed in 1859.

Here's how to crack it

Always pick the answer that seems the most obvious, and avoid thinking hard about answers that bring in new subject matter. This principle is similar to the concept of *scope* in the Reading section (see chapter 11).

EXCEPT/LEAST/NOT

You've seen these on standardized tests all your life, and, if you're like most people, you've gotten some of them wrong when you shouldn't have. The secret to EXCEPT/LEAST/NOT questions is to do them backward and use POE. For example, if the question is:

> The author would most likely agree with all
> of the following statements EXCEPT

History Bonus Answer

Thomas Jefferson died on July 4th, 1826. Spooky, huh?

Then you should (after figuring out what position the author is taking) go to answer choices and check off the ones he *would agree* with. One answer should be left, and that's the right answer. The reason it helps to do these questions backwards is that answering a question in the negative is about ten times harder than answering it in the positive. (That's why ETS frames them this way—it's a quick and easy way for them to guarantee a healthy number of people will get them wrong.)

It's a good idea to circle the EXCEPT or LEAST or NOT in the question as soon as you see it, to help you remember to do the question backward. The trap people fall into is that when they get to the answer choices, they wildly grab the first answer that matches the information in the passage or map, forgetting that they're supposed to look for the answer that *doesn't* match. We bet you never had a math test in which you were asked to pick the wrong answer—and effectively, that's what these questions ask you to do.

As you practice and analyze your mistakes, notice whether you miss a lot of EXCEPT/LEAST/NOT questions, make an extra effort to do them backward, and check off the choices with your pencil as you go along.

CARTOONS

It won't be Doonesbury, but it's better than nothing. You may see one on your test, and they'll most likely be political cartoons from this century. Treat them the same way you would a map or chart—study the cartoon carefully before even reading the question. Take note of anything written on it. Do you get it? What's the cartoon trying to say? Then go to the answers and use POE.

LAST WORDS . . .

On a recent test, a few of the Social Studies questions were pretty hard—you had to know not only who John Marshall was, but what his specific contributions to jurisprudence were. We want to stress that there are always going to be some fact-based questions you won't know the answer to. The best way to handle them is to guess quickly and move on. Don't give them a second thought. You can't know everything, but you can mess up your score by getting fixated and upset when you hit difficult questions.

CHAPTER 6—QUICK QUIZ ANSWERS

1. Franklin D. Roosevelt, in the 1930s. The New Deal was a legislative and administrative program that attempted social reform as well as economic recovery.

2. In laissez-faire capitalism, anything goes. The object is to allow economic success by avoiding any government regulation or interference.

3. Sociology: the study of societies, social institutions, and group behavior.

   Anthropology: the study of man, especially early or non-writing cultures.

   Demography: the study of population statistics.

4. The Depression began in October of 1929 when the stock market crashed and lasted into the 1930s. Herbert Hoover was president when it began, and Franklin Roosevelt was president when it ended.

5. Harry Truman ordered the atomic bomb dropped on Hiroshima and Nagasaki, believing it would end World War II, which it did.

6. Agrarianism was a political movement begun in the 1830s that supported farmers and land reform.

7. Sojourner Truth was freed from slavery in New York and became a powerful lecturer in support of abolition.

8. Socialism: an economic system in which resources and means of production are owned by the state as a means to correct the unfairness of capitalism.

   Progressivism: early twentieth-century movement aimed at reform—such as women's suffrage, improved working conditions, and abolishing child labor laws.

9. The Vietnam War.

10. A labor union.

11. Senator Joseph McCarthy was a maniac who screamed about communists infiltrating the U.S. During the McCarthy hearings, citizens were asked whether they were communists and whether their friends were communists. They were also forced to sign loyalty oaths.

Lord Knows

"Education makes a people easy to lead, but difficult to drive; easy to govern, but impossible to enslave."
— Lord Brougham

12. Kissinger was Secretary of State under Nixon.

13. The freedoms guaranteed by the Bill of Rights are: religion, press, speech, assembly, to bear arms, to submit to no unreasonable search and seizure, to a trial by jury, and not to incriminate yourself.

14. A nuclear family consists of two parents and two children.

15. Industrialization: the transformation of a culture to an economy that is characterized by factories and mechanization. Different parts of the world have become industrialized at different times, starting with the Industrial Revolution in Britain in the 18th century.

    Urbanization: the movement of the population from farms and rural communities to big cities.

    Imperialism: the domination of one country or culture over another.

16. Women's suffrage (the right to vote).

17. Strategic Arms Limitation Talks, undertaken by Nixon and Brehznev in 1972, in an effort to stabilize nuclear arms.

18. It began the process of desegregating American public school systems, by overturning the "separate but equal" provision of *Plessy v. Ferguson*.

19. Détente is an improvement in the relationship of two countries.

20. Inflation: the continuous rise of prices, sometimes caused by excess demand for products and sometimes by an increase in the cost of production.

7

Math

NUMBERS MAKE ME BREAK INTO A RASH . . .

We're not surprised. The majority of students stop taking math in high school. And for a lot of people, the memories of those math classes are rather distant, if not utterly unpleasant.

IN FACT, I'M FEELING ILL JUST THINKING ABOUT IT . . .

Well, cut it out. The math you need to know on the NTE is really very basic—SAT math is quite a bit more difficult. In this chapter, we'll teach you everything you need to know, along with some good strategies your math teacher probably never told you about. Who knows, you might end up wanting to teach math before we're finished.

Special section: How to study for math

1. It's sad but true—the only way to improve your math skills is to do a lot of practice problems (just like your math teacher used to tell you). So if you're weak on fractions, for example, do them every day until you've really got it down.

2. Take it one topic at a time. Start with arithmetic. Study it, practice it, learn it. Don't tackle algebra until you can do decimals and percentages in your sleep.

3. If you use a calculator regularly, put it away until after the test. You can't use it during the test, so you shouldn't be using one now. Drag those multiplication tables out from the cobwebs in the back of your mind. The more calculating you do on your own, the better.

4. Relax. More people are anxious about the math section than any other, so you're hardly alone. If you haven't studied math in years and years, you may be surprised at how easy it is now.

STATS—MATH SECTION

Number of questions: 25

Order of difficulty: yes

Question types: roughly 70% arithmetic; 20% first-year algebra; 10% geometry

Techniques: plugging in, ballparking

Bubbling: page by page

QUICK REVIEW

Arithmetic

The majority of the math questions are arithmetic questions, so this is the place to spend your study time.

Vocabulary

consecutive: numbers in order. Example: 1, 2, 3 are consecutive.

denominator: the bottom number of a fraction. Examples: for $\frac{1}{2}$, 2 is the denominator; for $\frac{3}{5}$, 5 is the denominator.

dividend: the number you're dividing into in a division problem. Example: in $9 \div 3$, the dividend is 9.

divisor: in a division problem, the number you're dividing by. Example: in $9 \div 3$, the divisor is 3.

even: a number evenly divisible by 2. Examples: 2, 4, 6, 8, 120, 14,322

factor: a divisor of a number. Examples: 2 is a factor of 6; 5 and 3 are factors of 15; 1, 2, 3, 4, 6, 8, 12, and 24 is the complete list of factors of 24.

multiple: a bigger number that a factor divides into. Examples: 6 is a multiple of 2; 15 is a multiple of both 3 and 5.

numerator: the top number of a fraction. Examples: for $\frac{5}{6}$, 5 is the numerator; for $\frac{8}{10}$, 8 is the numerator.

odd: a number not evenly divisible by 2. Examples: 1, 3, 5, 7, 12,845

product: the result when one number is multiplied by another. Example: in the operation $5 \times 4 = 20$, 20 is the product.

Numerology Can Be Fun!

1. Is your phone number an even or an odd number?
2. Do your phone number and your age have any factors in common?
3. If you add the numbers in your birthdate, is the resulting sum a multiple of your house or apartment number?

QUICK QUIZ

The answers are on page 51.

1. Name three multiples of 8.

2. What are the factors of 10?

3. How can you tell if a number is even?

FRACTIONS

To get a common denominator, pick a number that both denominators divide into evenly. The denominators of $\frac{2}{3}$ and $\frac{1}{4}$ are 3 and 4, which both go into 12.

So 12 is a common denominator for $\frac{2}{3}$ and $\frac{1}{4}$.

To add fractions, first multiply using the arrows, then add across the top and reduce:

$$\overset{10}{\underset{}{\frac{2}{5}}}\times\overset{5}{\underset{}{\frac{1}{5}}} = \frac{15}{25} = \frac{3}{5}$$

$$\overset{3}{\underset{}{\frac{1}{2}}}\times\overset{2}{\underset{}{\frac{1}{3}}} = \frac{5}{6}$$

Run Straight to the Nearest Bookstore

Get a copy of *Math Smart*, by Marcia Lerner. It explains every last detail of how to do basic math, and manages not to be in the least bit boring. If you want more, look for *Math Smart II*, also by Marcia Lerner.

To subtract fractions, find a common denominator and subtract across the top:

$$\frac{7}{9} - \frac{4}{9} = \frac{3}{9} = \frac{1}{3}$$

$$\frac{7}{8} - \frac{1}{4} = \frac{7}{8} - \frac{2}{8} = \frac{5}{8}$$

To multiply fractions, reduce if possible, then multiply across the top and the bottom:

$$\frac{3}{4} \times \frac{3}{5} = \frac{9}{20}$$

$$\frac{6}{7} \times \frac{1}{4} = \frac{3}{14}$$

To divide fractions, flip the second fraction, and then follow the rules for multiplying:

$$\frac{1}{5} \div \frac{1}{3} = \frac{1}{5} \times \frac{3}{3} = \frac{3}{5}$$

$$\frac{4}{3} \div \frac{5}{6} = \frac{4}{3} \times \frac{6}{5} = \frac{8}{5}$$

To figure out which of two fractions is bigger, use the bowtie method. Cross-multiply starting at the bottom and crossing to the top. The side with the bigger product is the bigger fraction.

Which is bigger, $\frac{5}{7}$ or $\frac{8}{11}$?

$$\overset{55}{\underset{}{\frac{5}{7}}}\times\overset{56}{\underset{}{\frac{8}{11}}}$$

56 is bigger than 55, so $\frac{8}{11}$ is bigger.

QUICK QUIZ

The answers are on page 51.

1. $\dfrac{1}{2} + \dfrac{3}{4} =$

2. $\dfrac{1}{3} \times \dfrac{2}{5} =$

3. $\dfrac{1}{4} \div \dfrac{1}{2} =$

4. $\dfrac{2}{3} - \dfrac{1}{2} =$

5. $\dfrac{3}{8} \times \dfrac{1}{9} =$

DECIMALS

To add or subtract decimals, line them up by the decimal point and add or subtract as usual:

$$
\begin{array}{r}
10.365 \\
+\ 1.02 \\
\hline
11.385
\end{array}
\qquad
\begin{array}{r}
5.062 \\
+\ .05 \\
\hline
5.012
\end{array}
$$

To multiply decimals, first multiply as usual:

$$
\begin{array}{r}
6.2 \\
\times\ 3.5 \\
\hline
310 \\
186 \\
\hline
2170
\end{array}
$$

Then count up the number of digits in the problem to the right of the decimal point:

$$
\begin{array}{r}
6\,②\\
\times\ 3\,⑤ \longrightarrow 2
\end{array}
$$

And put the same number of digits to the right of the decimal point in the product:

$$21.70$$

To divide decimals: If only the dividend has a decimal, move the decimal into place and divide as usual:

$$
\begin{array}{r}
3.2 \\
4\,\overline{)12.8}
\end{array}
$$

If the divisor has a decimal point, move the decimal point to the right until the divisor is an integer:

$$1.5\,\overline{)6} \longrightarrow 15.\,\overline{)6}$$

Drill to Do at Home Alone:

Working With Fractions
1. Order a pizza.
2. Eat a slice.
3. Calculate what fractional part of the pizza you just ate, and what fractional part remains.
4. Eat another slice.
5. Repeat Step 3.
6. Repeat Step 2 followed by Step 3 until pizza box is empty.

Then move the decimal point of the dividend the same number of places:

$$15\,\overline{)\,60.}$$

Then divide as usual:

$$\begin{array}{r} 4. \\ 15\,\overline{)\,60.} \end{array}$$

Another Drill to Do at Home Alone:

Working With Decimals

1. Find loose change under sofa cushions and car seats.
2. Find more loose change on top of bureau and in pants pockets.
3. Put coins in random piles of five coins each.
4. Add value of coins in each pile.
5. Divide value of the first pile into that of the second pile. Add the values of the third and fourth piles, etc.
6. After you have practiced multiplying, dividing, subtracting, and adding the piles, spend the money on something really good, like Dove bars.

QUICK QUIZ

The answers are on page 52.

1. $2.02 + 60.18 =$
2. $5.132 - .05 =$
3. $6.32 \times 3.2 =$
4. $12.6 \div 2 =$
5. $24 \div 1.2 =$

PERCENTAGES

To convert a percentage to a decimal, move the decimal point two spaces to the left:

$$50\% = .5$$
$$5\% = .05$$
$$100\% = 1$$
$$.06\% = .0006$$

To convert a decimal to a percentage, move the decimal point two spaces to the right:

$$.20 = 20\%$$
$$.35 = 35\%$$
$$.08 = 8\%$$
$$1.2 = 120\%$$

To convert a percentage to a fraction, put the number over 100:

$$25\% = \frac{25}{100}$$

$$7\% = \frac{7}{100}$$

$$98\% = \frac{98}{100}$$

$$110\% = \frac{110}{100}$$

44 ◆ CRACKING THE PRAXIS II: NTE

To get the percentage of a number, multiply by the decimal:

$$40\% \text{ of } 10 = .4 \times 10 = 4$$
$$5\% \text{ of } 20 = .05 \times 20 = 1$$

[handwritten: 50% of 20 = .5 × 20 = 10]

To solve a percentage word problem, transform the sentence into an equation by substituting:

× for *of*

= for *is*

x for *what*

the fraction for the percent

For example:

> Sally spends 25 percent of her weekly salary on Ring-Dings. If she makes $400 a week, how much does she spend on Ring-Dings?

[handwritten: 25% .25 × 400]

So Sally spent 25% of her $400 salary, which transforms to $\frac{25}{100} \times 400 = x$, so $x = 100$. Or you can do what we showed you above, and just multiply by the decimal: $.25 \times 400 = 100$

Quick Quiz

The answers are on page 52.

1. What is the fractional equivalent of 15%? *[handwritten: 15/100]*

2. What is the decimal equivalent of 15%? *[handwritten: .15]*

3. What is 15% of 200? *[handwritten: .15 × 200 or 15/100 × 200/1 = 30]*

4. What is 30% of 200? *[handwritten: 30/100 × 200/1 = 60]*

5. What is 1.5 written as a percent? *[handwritten: 150%]*

Proportions

To set up a proportion, match categories on the top and bottom, then cross-multiply. For example:

> If 6 bananas cost 50 cents, how much do 30 bananas cost?

$$\text{(bananas)} \quad \frac{6}{50} = \frac{30}{x} \quad \text{(cents)}$$

[handwritten: 6x = 50 × 30 = 6x, 1500 = 6x, x = 250, 1500/6 = 6x/6]

To solve it, just cross-multiply. $6x = 50 \times 30$, so $6x = 1,500$, and $x = 250$ cents, or $2.50. It doesn't matter whether you put the bananas on top or the cents—you only have to make sure that the bananas are either both on top or both on the bottom.

Drills to Do Outside the Home

Working With Percentages

1. Go shopping, but only to stores advertising sales such as "20% Off!!!"
2. Browse through the store, calculating how much actual money you would save if you bought discounted items.

or

1. Have dinner in a restaurant every night for a week.
2. Calculate the tip (no guessing, asking a friend, or using a calculator).

Quick Quiz

The answers are on page 53.

1. If 20 nails cost 5 cents, how much do 200 nails cost?

2. If a car can drive 300 miles on one tank of gas, how far can it drive if the tank is only $\frac{1}{4}$ full?

3. If a 10 foot tall tree casts a shadow that's 4 feet long, how long is the shadow for an 8 foot tree?

Scary Proportion Drill

If it takes you 20 seconds to read your horoscope each day, approximately how much time will you spend reading your horoscope over the next 20 years? (Hint: 20 years is roughly 7,300 days.)

Ratios

A ratio is just a comparison—it tells you how many of one thing you have compared to how many of another thing you have. For example, if you have just eaten cookies and Milk Duds in a ratio of 3 to 2, that means you've eaten 3 cookies for every 2 Milk Duds. By itself, the ratio doesn't tell you the total number of things involved—you could have eaten 5 things or 50 things (you pig!).

To figure the actual numbers in a ratio, add the numbers in the ratio and divide that number into the total. Then take that number and multiply by both parts of the ratio.

There are 35 people in a room, with men and women in a ratio of 2:3. How many women are in the room?

First add the numbers in the ratio: 2 + 3 = 5. Now divide the total number of people by 5: 35 ÷ 5 = 7. Multiply that number by both parts: 7 × 2 = 14 men, and 7 × 3 = 21 women. Notice that 14 and 21 add up to the total of 35.

One more thing. You'll get the answer wrong if you mix up the order in the ratio—if the problem says men to women in a ratio of 2:3, the first number is men and the second is women, not the other way around.

Seem complicated? It seems worse than it is. It just takes a little dedicated practice.

Quick Quiz

The answers are on page 53.

1. There are 12 pieces of fruit in a bowl, with a ratio of apples and pears being 1:3. How many pears are in the bowl?

2. A tray holds chocolate and vanilla cupcakes in a ratio of 5 to 2. If there are 28 cupcakes in all, how many cupcakes are chocolate?

BALLPARKING

A very good way to avoid careless mistakes is to estimate your answer before working it out. A ballpark figure allows you to eliminate some choices before continuing to do the problem. You might even get lucky and eliminate all but one answer!

Eliminate at least one answer from the following by ballparking:

1. Which fraction is smallest?

(A) $\dfrac{14}{15}$

(B) $\dfrac{3}{4}$

(C) $\dfrac{4}{5}$

(D) $\dfrac{3}{2}$

(E) $\dfrac{99}{100}$

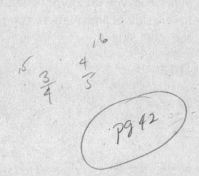

pg 42

Here's how to crack it

You're looking for something small. Let's evaluate the answers: (A) and (E) are close to 1, and (D) is bigger than 1. Eliminate all of them, and you're left with (B) and (C). Not bad for a few seconds' work. Now you can use the bowtie to find which is smaller if you can't tell by looking at them—the answer is (B).

ALGEBRA

Solving for x

Keep in mind, this is only basic algebra. You were doing this when you were just a wee pup. Let's try one:

$$4x + 10 = 30$$

Since we're solving for x, the first thing to do is to isolate it by moving the 10 to the other side of the equals sign. To do that, subtract 10 from both sides.

$$
\begin{array}{r}
4x + 10 = 30 \\
-10 \quad -10 \\
\hline
4x \qquad = 20
\end{array}
$$

Almost there. Now we have to get rid of the 4, so divide both sides by 4:

$$\frac{4x}{4} = \frac{20}{4}$$
$$x = 5$$

To check it, substitute 5 in for the x in the original equation:

$$(4)(5) + 10 = 30$$
$$20 + 10 = 30$$
$$30 = 30$$

Is it all coming back to you? We hope so. As you practice the equations, just keep the following rules in mind:

1. To solve for a variable (x, b, f, or whatever), isolate the variable on one side of the equals sign.

2. Whenever you do anything (add, subtract, multiply, or divide) to one side of an equation, you must do the exact same thing to the other side.

QUICK QUIZ

1. $2d - 6 = 2$

2. $\dfrac{x}{4} = \dfrac{7}{2}$

3. $6t - 4 = t + 1$

PLUGGING IN

The trouble with algebra is that hardly anyone uses it in real life. When you balance your checkbook, pay a bill, or leave a tip, you're using arithmetic, not algebra.

For that reason, you're probably a lot more comfortable with numbers than with variables. So on some NTE problems, try substituting numbers for the variables and work out the problem from there. Here's one to try:

If g is half of y, then

(A) y is half of g

(B) g multiplied by $\dfrac{1}{2}$ equals y

(C) g plus $\dfrac{1}{2}$ equals y

(D) y is twice g

(E) y is two more than g

Variable Interest

Don't let a variable scare you —it simply represents the number you don't know (yet).

Here's how to crack it

Instead of getting confused by the ys and gs, let's turn them into numbers. All we have to do is choose numbers that satisfy the requirements of the question: let's say $g = 3$, so then $y = 6$. (3 is half of 6.) Now let's go to the answers. When we plug in our numbers, (A) says 6 is half of 3—cross it out. (B) says 3 multiplied by

$\frac{1}{2}$ = 6. That's false too, so cross it out. (C) says 3 plus $\frac{1}{2}$ = 6; (E) says 6 is 2 more than 3—cross them both out. The right answer, (D), says 6 is twice 3, which is the only true statement in the bunch.

THAT'S COOL! SO WHEN CAN I USE PLUGGING IN?

Look for variables in both the question and the answer choices. The problems usually concern factors or multiples or will look like the problem we just solved above.

QUICK QUIZ

The answers are on page 54.

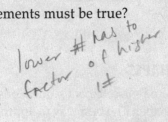

1. If $3x = y$, then x is

    (A) bigger than y
    (B) three times y
    (C) one-third y
    (D) three more than y
    (E) three less than y

    P is a multiple of Q
    2 and 5 are factors of Q

2. Which of the following statements must be true?

    (A) 10 is a factor of P
    (B) P is a factor of Q
    (C) $2 \times 5 = P$
    (D) $PQ = 10$
    (E) 7 is a factor of Q

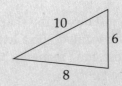

lower # has to factor of higher #

GEOMETRY

The geometry questions on the NTE aren't about proofs and theorems, or even about complex shapes like cones and spheres that require knowing a lot of formulas. You probably had this stuff in the sixth grade.

PERIMETER

The perimeter is simply the distance around a shape, like the length of a fence around a garden.

To find the perimeter, add up the sides.

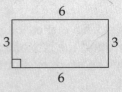

perimeter: 18   perimeter: 24

Working With Geometry

1. Measure the dimensions of your bedroom.
2. What is its perimeter?
3. How many square feet does it have?
4. Measure the dimensions of your closet and calculate the square footage.
5. How many closets could fit into your bedroom?

RECTANGLES AND SQUARES

To find the area of a square or rectangle, multiply the length times the width. (For a square, the number will be the same)

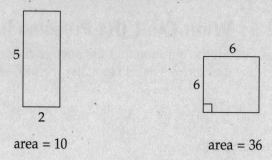

area = 10   area = 36

TRIANGLES

To find the area of a triangle, multiply the base times the height and then divide the result by 2. (A = (bh)/2)

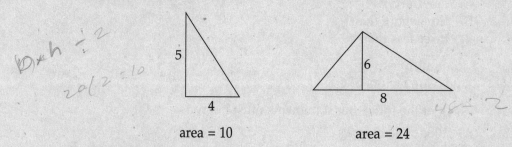

area = 10   area = 24

FUNNY SHAPES

You'll see some miscellaneous questions asking about various shapes and how they fold together. The best way to approach them is to take a deep breath and try to visualize the object as best you can. Pretend you are holding the object in your hand. Take your time getting a feel for the shape of it rather than jumping to the answer choices. And if you hate this type of question, guess and move on.

QUICK QUIZ

The answers are on page 54.

1. How many feet of fencing would be required to enclose a garden measuring 40 feet by 30 feet?

2. Jeannie wants to carpet her bedroom, which measures 12 feet by 14 feet. How many square feet of carpet does she need?

3. A gift box in the shape of a cube has sides 5 inches long. If Bob wants to tie a length of ribbon around the box one time, how many inches of ribbon does he need, excluding the knot?

CRACKING THE QUESTIONS

1. Don't rush. Lots of people think speed is the key to doing well on standardized tests, but you know better. If you can handle the math required for a particular problem, make sure you spend enough time on it to get it right.

2. Don't do math problems in your head. Write everything down. You won't earn any extra points for having a clean test booklet, so scribble all over it.

3. One thing at a time. Sometimes math questions require more than one step. Don't try to do two things at once, or the chances of making a careless error go up astronomically.

4. Read the question carefully. If the question asks for the area, don't calculate the perimeter. If the question asks for y, don't solve for x. It's easy to do the wrong thing if you're tearing through the section at breakneck speed. Slow down and spend some concentrated time making sure you're answering the right question.

5. Check your computations. The best way to do this is to do them over again, in a separate corner of your test booklet. Don't simply glance at your past work. For some reason, when people stare at a finished computation, their eyes glaze over and they miss mistakes. (It's happened to the best of us.)

CHAPTER 7—QUICK QUIZ ANSWERS

Vocabulary

1. 8, 16, 24, 32, 40 . . . any number that 8 goes into evenly is a multiple of 8

2. 1, 2, 5, 10

3. An even number always ends in an even number. So 17,952 is even, while 28,463 is not.

Fractions

1. $\dfrac{1}{2} + \dfrac{3}{4} = \dfrac{2}{4} + \dfrac{3}{4} = \dfrac{5}{4}$

2. $\dfrac{1}{3} \times \dfrac{2}{5} = \dfrac{2}{15}$

3. $\dfrac{1}{4} \div \dfrac{1}{2} = \dfrac{1}{4} \times \dfrac{2}{1} = \dfrac{2}{4} = \dfrac{1}{2}$

4. $\dfrac{2}{3} - \dfrac{1}{2} = \dfrac{4}{6} - \dfrac{3}{6} = \dfrac{1}{6}$

5. $\dfrac{\cancel{3}^{1}}{8} \times \dfrac{1}{\cancel{9}_{3}} = \dfrac{1}{24}$

Decimals

1.
$$\begin{array}{r} 2.02 \\ + 60.18 \\ \hline 62.20 \end{array}$$

2.
$$\begin{array}{r} 5.132 \\ - .05 \\ \hline 5.082 \end{array}$$

3.
$$\begin{array}{r} 6.32 \\ \times 3.2 \\ \hline 1264 \\ 1896 \\ \hline 20.224 \end{array}$$

4. $2\overline{)12.6}$ with quotient 6.3

5. $1.2\overline{)24}$ $12.\overline{)240.}$ with quotient $20.$

Percents

1. $\dfrac{15}{100}$

2. Move the decimal point 2 places to the left. The answer is .15

3. Multiply 200 by .15 to get 30

4. Multiply 200 by .3 to get 60

5. Move the decimal point 2 places to the right. The answer is 150%

Proportions

1. $\dfrac{5}{20} = \dfrac{x}{200}$

   $20x = 1{,}000$

   $x = 50$

2. $\dfrac{300}{1} = \dfrac{x}{\frac{1}{4}}$

   $x = 300\left(\dfrac{1}{4}\right)$

   $x = 75$

3. $\dfrac{10}{4} = \dfrac{8}{x}$

   $32 = 10x$

   $x = 3.2$

Ratios

1. 9. Add the numbers in the ratio (1 + 3 = 4) and divide that number into the total (4 into 12 is 3). Now multiply that number by the pear part of the ratio (3 × 3) and you get 9 pears. (There are also 3 apples, not that anyone asked.)

2. 20. Add the numbers in the ratio (5 + 2 = 7), divide into the total (7 into 28 = 4) and multiply by the chocolate part of the ratio (4 × 5 = 20 chocolate cupcakes).

Solving for x

1. $2d - 6 = 2$

   $2d = 8$

   $d = 4$

2. $\dfrac{x}{4} = \dfrac{7}{2}$

   $28 = 2x$

   $14 = x$

   $\dfrac{28}{2} = \dfrac{2x}{2}$

   $14 = x$

3. $6t - 4 = t + 1$

   $5t = 5$

   $t = 1$

Plugging in

1. **(C)**. Let's plug in 2 for *x* and 6 for *y*. Go ahead and write a 6 next to all the *y*s in the answer choices just to make eliminating easier. Is 2 bigger than 6? Cross out (A). Is 2 three times 6? Cross out (B). Is 2 three more than 6? Cross out (D). Is 2 three less than 6? Cross out (E).

2. **(A)**. Plug in for *Q* first—it has to have factors of 2 and 5, so let's make it 10. If *P* is a multiple of 10, let's make it 20. Now for the answers. If you plug in 10 for *Q* and 20 for *P*, the only statement that's true is (A).

Geometry

1. 140 feet. Draw yourself a picture, labeling two sides 40 and two sides 30. Now add up all the sides. That's it. (If you thought the answer was 1200, you calculated the area. Read the question more carefully.)

2. 168. To get square feet, you need to calculate the area, which is simply length times width, or 12×14. If you multiplied 12 times 14 but got the wrong answer, be more careful with your computations. Double-check them. (We know you didn't try to do it in your head.)

3. 20. Try to visualize the ribbon going around the box. How many sides must the ribbon go around? Four. So if each side is 5 inches, Bob needs $5 \times 4 = 20$ inches.

8

Literature
and Fine Arts

If you were an art history or an English major, spend most of your time studying something else. If you weren't, don't despair, because you don't really need to know much in the way of specific facts for this section. For example, you won't be asked to match the author to the quote, identify movements, or name the painting or the artist.

STATS—LITERATURE AND FINE ARTS SECTION

Number of questions: 35

Percentage of fact-based questions: strictly speaking, about 10%

Order of difficulty: no

Question types: Literature: 16–17 questions asking for analysis of poetry or fiction excerpts; Fine Arts: 16–17 questions asking for analysis of paintings, architecture, and photographs; Music: 1–3 questions asking for analysis or specific knowledge of music

Techniques: POE

Bubbling: page by page

I. LITERATURE

Your primary job on Literature questions is to read carefully and, of course, use POE. Some knowledge of terms and vocabulary will be useful.

QUICK REVIEW

Achilles, Agamemnon, Odysseus, Dido, Patroclus, Oedipus: all characters from Greek epics

allusion: a reference, usually to an earlier literary work

analogy: a comparison

animate/inanimate: living/not living; a dog is animate, a table is inanimate

apprehensive: fearful of what's to come; wary

assonance: not quite rhyme, but a similarity of sound in two words resulting from the vowel; for example, *love* and *bug*, *mean* and *leap*, *loose* and *boot*

blank verse: unrhymed iambic pentameter; most of Shakespeare is written in blank verse

cynical: distrustful and disbelieving in people's integrity

ephemeral: fleeting; short-lived

epic: a long narrative poem that tells the story of a hero; for example, the *Iliad* and the *Odyssey*

fable: a story that has a moral point

irony: the use of words to convey the opposite of the literal meaning

Mars, Mercury, Juno, Pluto, Jupiter, Diana: all Roman gods

metaphor: a figure of speech used to make a comparison; for example, *My love life is a desert*.

meter: a rhythmic pattern in poetry, such as iambic pentameter

narrative: any kind of writing that tells a story

onomatopoeia: when the sound of a word suggests its meaning; for example, *sizzle, meow, squish*

point of view: the standpoint from which a story is written, such as first person or third person. First-person stories are written from only one character's point of view; for example, *I was a happy child*.

protagonist: the main character in a story

rhyme scheme: a pattern of end rhymes, such as ABAB (meaning that the 1st and 3rd lines rhyme, and the 2nd and 4th rhyme).

simile: a figure of speech used to make a comparison. A simile is slightly different from a metaphor because it makes the comparison more overt by using a word such as *like*; for example, *Your eyes are like mud puddles*.

secular: earthly; temporal; not religious

transitory: not permanent; for example, *Our love is but a transitory pleasure . . .*

Zeus, Hera, Poseidon, Apollo, Athena, Aphrodite: all Greek gods

CRACKING THE QUESTIONS

1. Read the question first. There's usually only one or two questions per excerpt—it's better to read them first so that when you go back to the excerpt you'll know what you're looking for.

2. The questions are of two types: general and specific. General questions ask something about the excerpt as a whole, and specific questions ask about particular lines. Do the general questions first. Answer the question in your own words *before* you look at the answer choices, and then use POE.

Fruits and Vegetables

"Training is everything. The peach was once a bitter almond; cauliflower is nothing but cabbage with a college education."
— Mark Twain

Let's try one:

> Sarah is lurking through the house. She creeps down the long back staircase, concentrating on the creaky spots. There is a dark stain on one step that Sarah believes is blood: it's a wide, flat shape, made by something thick spilled on the wood.
>
> In the first floor hallway she edges up on the kitchen, can hear Velly ironing. The Coke bottle fitted with a nozzle, water being shook down on the clothes. She stands in the hallway, her hands against the wainscoting, the ridges of dark wood. Sarah loves listening in.
>
> Almost always it's the small chores she listens in on. Her father neatening up the coal bin, her mother pouring a drink. Sarah waits for someone to slip, to say or do something that will give them away. She doesn't think of giving herself away; she is watching the others.

> Which of the following is the best description of Sarah?
>
> (A) She longs to escape her house and family.
>
> (B) She is furtive and guilty of stealing small objects from other members of the household.
>
> (C) She is imaginative and sensitive to the world around her.
>
> (D) She is a troubled and angry child although not usually badly behaved.
>
> (E) She is trying to avoid doing her share of the household chores.

Here's how to crack it

Read the question first, then the passage. Then, before looking at the answers, ask yourself to describe Sarah. What does the passage tell you? She's sneaking around the house, noticing things. Now look at the answers, and remember to look for anything that makes an answer wrong. (A) "longs to escape"? That's not mentioned. (B) she's certainly furtive, but keep reading—there's no mention of her stealing anything. (C) hey—there's nothing wrong with this answer! (D) "troubled," maybe—but "angry"? It's not in the passage. And neither is (E).

You can see from our explanation that you should base your answer only on what is explicitly in the passage. Don't make assumptions, don't imagine beyond what is given.

Now let's try a specific question about the same passage:

In the third sentence, the author implies that
- (A) Sarah had spilled something on the back stairs
- (B) the stain on the wood was probably not caused by blood
- (C) Sarah's household was a violent one
- (D) the house was not kept very clean
- (E) Sarah's parents could not afford to carpet the stairs

Here's how to crack it

First, reread the first paragraph. (When a question asks about a specific line, it's often helpful to read around it to get the context.) Can you answer the question before looking at the answers? Notice the words *believes* and *something* in that paragraph. Is the author telling us the stain really is blood, or is she telling us that Sarah has a big imagination? (That's what's known as a leading question.) Yes, (B) is the right answer—although you didn't have to figure that out for yourself. You could get it right by eliminating the other answers, all of which include something that wasn't implied by the passage.

Last words . . .

If English was never your strong suit, go through the section and do all the Fine Arts and Music questions first. If poetry makes no sense to you, "skip" them and do the fiction passages first. And just remember that the secret to answering Literature questions is to focus on the excerpts themselves and not to stray away from what the lines say. Don't infer, don't imagine, don't get creative.

II. Fine Arts

None of the Fine Arts questions will ask you to identify a work of art or its creator. Instead, they ask you to analyze its composition or meaning—either of which you can do without any special training or knowledge of art history.

You'll be shown a picture of some kind—a photograph, painting, sculpture, or building—and asked to describe it in some way. For several questions, you'll be given five pictures and then asked two or three questions about the group.

Typical Questions

The costumes of the dancers in the photograph above serve to . . .

Which of the following is an important feature of the painting above?

Which of the following causes the building in the picture above to appear to reach toward the sky?

Pope is Dope

"A little learning is a dangerous thing."
— Alexander Pope

Now let's give this one a try:

Go to the nearest art museum and wander around the paintings and sculpture. Don't worry about who did what and when, just pay attention visually. What kind of mood does the art evoke? What's the composition like? What part is your eye most drawn to?

Which of the following serves to emphasize the sorrowful nature of the painting shown above?

(A) Some of the subjects are smiling, and others are frowning.

(B) The subjects are dressed in tattered clothing and apparently have no means of financial support.

(C) The church spire in the background leads the viewer's eye upward, just as many of the subjects are looking upward.

(D) The composition is based on a series of circles that overlap each other.

(E) The composition is based on a line that starts at the top and moves steadily downward, cutting the painting diagonally and ending at the bottom.

Here's how to crack it

First, just look at the painting. What do you notice? A line of unhappy men that proceeds from the top left and moves to the bottom right. Next read the question. We're looking for an answer that emphasizes sorrow and that matches what you see in the painting. In (A), there aren't any smiling subjects. Eliminate it. In (B), their clothing doesn't look particularly tattered—eliminate it. In (C), the viewer's eye is really led downward, because that downward line of men is the strongest element in the painting. And why would "looking upward" emphasize sorrow? Eliminate it. In (D), if there are any circles, you'd have to look for them with a microscope. The main elements are triangles (all of the buildings in the background as well as the two triangles formed by that line of men crossing the painting). And again, what do circles have to do with sorrow? Eliminate (D). In (E), the description matches what you see in the painting—there is a line that starts at the top left and cuts diagonally across the painting to the bottom right. And descent is an appropriate metaphor for sorrow, so the answer is (E).

Notice that you could get this question right simply by comparing the answer choices to the painting and seeing which one matches the best. You don't really need to know any special art history jargon or have had any special training. Just trust your eyes, use POE, and make sure to give the artwork a good look before you start worrying about answering the question.

QUICK REVIEW

The following words show up in both questions and answer choices. Make sure you understand what they mean.

abstract: a style of painting that doesn't attempt pictorial representation (in other words, you can't tell exactly what you're looking at)

asymmetrical: not evenly balanced; not symmetrical

composition: the arrangement of elements in an artwork; for example, a composition might be based on a triangle, with two objects at the bottom and one at the top

contrast: the juxtaposition of elements, which emphasizes their difference; for example, dark areas in a photograph might contrast with light areas

facade: the front of a building (or any side that has particular architectural interest)

foreground: the part of a painting or photograph that's nearest to the viewer

geometrical: having geometric shape; look for squares, triangles, circles, and lines

horizontal: going from side to side (like the horizon); opposite of vertical

juxtaposition: putting two things close to each other

massive: huge, immense

ornate: highly decorated

perspective: artistic technique that makes something one-dimensional appear three-dimensional

stylized: characterized by a particular style rather than being simply representational

symmetrical: balanced; two sides are a mirror image of each other

vertical: going up and down (like a pine tree); opposite of horizontal

Cracking the questions

All Fine Arts questions ask for some kind of description, so you should focus on the answer choices—we mean, of course, using POE.

1. Read the question first. The question may direct you to a specific part of the picture. Don't waste time gazing at the picture until you know what exactly to pay attention to.

2. Study the picture. Did the question ask about composition? Then look carefully at the way the elements in the picture are arranged. Did the question ask about facial expressions? Then study them closely. Focus your attention only on whatever part of the picture the question is asking about.

3. Go to the answer choices and eliminate. Don't worry if you don't see a great-looking answer right off the bat—as usual, the best way to approach these questions is by eliminating answers one by one. Remember that even one word can make an answer choice wrong.

4. If you've never taken a single art course and wouldn't go to a museum unless you were tied up and dragged, don't be discouraged. The Fine Arts questions really aren't very jargony, and if you are conscientious about eliminating, you'll get a whole lot of them correct—whether you know your Picasso or not.

9

Science

Questions in the science section encompass physics, chemistry, geology, astronomy, meteorology, and biology—with about half the questions on the latter. The good news is that you can get a majority of the questions right by knowing a pretty small amount of science; many of the questions require only the kind of science knowledge you get by reading the newspaper or *TIME* magazine, not by in-depth study of even a high school textbook.

SO I DON'T HAVE TO STUDY?

Well, let's not get carried away. Along with diligent use of POE, there are a few terms and concepts that you should know. So spend some time on the following review, and the science section should be a piece of cake.

STATS—SCIENCE SECTION

Number of questions: 30

Percentage of fact-based questions: approximately 50%

Order of difficulty: yes

Question types: some Roman numeral, some charts, some EXCEPT/LEAST/NOT

Techniques: POE; avoid extreme language

Bubbling: page by page

QUICK REVIEW

Biology

amino acids: adenine, guanine, thymine, and cytosine (components of DNA)

bacteria: tiny cellular organisms, some of which cause disease (tetanus, strep throat) and some of which are useful (cheese making, sewage treatment)

cell: the smallest unit of living matter

cell membrane: the outer "skin" (or layer) of a cell. For most cells, some materials can pass through the membrane and others cannot, which makes the membrane selectively permeable

classification system: (in order, from largest to smallest) Kingdom, Phylum, Class, Order, Family, Genus, Species

coniferous: cone-bearing trees that don't lose their leaves in winter, such as pine and spruce (they usually have needles instead of leaves)

cytoplasm: the goop inside a cell

deciduous: trees that lose their leaves in winter, such as maple and elm

DNA: genetic information located in the nucleus of every cell, composed of amino acids

evolutionary order: (from earliest appearance to latest) invertebrates, fish, amphibians, reptiles, mammals, human beings

fibrovascular bundles: consist of the xylem and phloem, which are tubes that carry water and food to the different parts of a plant

meiosis: nuclear division of a cell, resulting in half the number of chromosomes

mitochondria: little sausagelike units that float around in the cytoplasm; the powerhouses of a cell, where energy (ATP) is produced from nutrients

mitosis: nuclear division of a cell, producing an exact replica of the parent cell

nucleus: the central body within a cell, responsible for important functions such as reproduction

photosynthesis: the process by which plants use the sun's energy to make food from water and carbon dioxide

renewable resource: an energy source, such as sunlight, that won't eventually be used up

sexual reproduction: always involves the fusion of two gametes (sperm and egg)

viruses: tiny particles that attack other cells; responsible for diseases such as typhoid, polio, malaria, and chickenpox, some of which have been nearly eradicated by vaccines

Chemistry

atom: the smallest unit of matter, consisting of a nucleus and orbiting electrons; made up of neutrons and protons and has a positive charge

atomic number: the number of electrons in an atom

CO_2: carbon dioxide

element: a substance that can't be divided into simpler substances; for example oxygen, carbon, or helium

isotope: atoms of the same element with a different number of neutrons in the nucleus (the number of protons and electrons will be the same)

neutron: an uncharged part of an atomic nucleus

proton: a positively charged part of an atomic nucleus

states of matter: comes in only three forms—solids, liquids, or gases

Physics

force: something that causes an object to move; main forces are gravitational, electromagnetic, and nuclear

Fit and Trim

Darwin is responsible for the concept of "survival of the fittest"; his ship was *The Beagle*.

frequency: the number of waves produced in one second

kinetic energy: energy of motion

potential energy: stored energy not yet in use

wavelength: different kinds of energy travel in waves, such as light and sound; wavelength is just a measure of the length of one of these waves

Geology

continental drift: the theory that most of the land on Earth was originally one land mass and gradually split apart. The splitting is caused by plate tectonics.

igneous: type of rock formed from cooled lava, or volcanic rock

metamorphic: type of rock formed when sedimentary or igneous rock is exposed to extreme heat or pressure

sedimentary: type of rock formed when rock is moved (by a glacier, for example) and then settles and consolidates back into rock (such as sandstone)

tectonic plates: slow-moving pieces of the Earth's crust

Meteorology

front: the meeting of two air masses of different humidity and temperature

Astronomy

axis: a straight line through a planet or moon that the planet or moon rotates about

black hole: result of the gravitational collapse of a huge star; matter is pulled into it and can't escape

planets of our solar system: (in order, starting from closest to the sun) Mercury, Venus, Earth, Mars, Jupiter, Saturn, Uranus, Neptune, and Pluto

red giant: late stage in the evolution of a star

revolution: when a planet or moon travels once around in its orbit, that's one revolution

rotation: when a planet or moon spins once around on its axis, that's one rotation

General concepts

Scientists confirm a **hypothesis,** or educated guess, by using the **scientific method**. Scientific method is used as a way to eliminate the various possible causes of a particular effect.

For example, if a scientist hypothesized that a certain species of beetle could be killed with vinegar, she might introduce vinegar to several boxes containing the beetles and also keep some boxes of beetles without vinegar as a control group. The scientist must try to make sure all other conditions are the same, so that if the vinegared beetles die, she is as certain as possible that they did not die from some other cause.

An experiment needs to be repeated at least several times and produce the same results for the hypothesis to be confirmed, since there's always a possibility that the results are simply a coincidence.

Cracking the answer choices

The question types in the Science section are pretty straightforward, so you'll want to focus your attention on eliminating answer choices.

Although some questions require you to know specific facts, a lot of them don't. You can get them right just by using POE and your common sense.

Let's try one. Never mind the question—which answers can you eliminate?

(A) The best solution to the problem of toxic waste is to make producing it or disposing of it punishable by long prison terms and multi-million-dollar fines.

(B) It is often less expensive to control air pollution than water pollution.

(C) Damage to the environment caused by chemical dumping can take decades to overcome if measures are not taken to contain it.

(D) To combat illegal dumping, every community should have a toxic waste dump nearby so that it is easily accessible to anyone wishing to dispose of hazardous material.

(E) Certain states have historically allowed toxic material from other states to be transported there for disposal, although such states are increasingly unwilling to continue the practice.

Remember:

First pass: easy questions.

Second pass: questions you kinda-sorta know.

Third pass: bubble in your pre-selected answer.

Here's how to crack it

We hope you crossed out (A) and (D)—the NTE is never going to advocate such extreme measures. (So you've got some lead paint in your old house? Off to prison with you, and by the way, fork over a few mil while you're at it!)

Correct answers will generally be mild, somewhat PC, and difficult to dispute—which means they may not jump out at you. If, using your common sense, you are pretty sure an answer choice is a true statement—like choices (C) and (E)—don't cross it out. But don't choose it unless it answers the specific question asked.

Always work by using POE: Never try to justify how an answer could be right. *Look for what could be wrong with it.*

YOU'RE THE BEST, MOST, EVERY, ALL, ONLY ONE FOR ME

You may have noticed in the example above that some choices used strong, absolute language (like *best* and *should*), and some used milder, weaker, qualified language (like *often* and *increasingly*). Generally speaking, avoid the extreme stuff. Why? Because an extreme statement is harder to prove.

Which statement is more likely to be true?

> I always floss my teeth before I go to bed.
> I usually floss my teeth before I go to bed.

The problem with the first statement is that if only one time in your whole life you fell asleep on the sofa and didn't wake up until morning, the entire statement is false. The second statement is harder to pin down—*usually* could mean six times a week or four times a week, and the statement is true either way.

Scientists like things to be exact. And what that means is that definitive statements of truth are kind of rare—so you should avoid picking them.

To make things simpler, we've come up with the following lists.

Words to Love: some, may, can, associated with, not necessarily, might, many

Words to Avoid: best, only, causes, solely, every, all, always

But Wait . . .

On an EXCEPT/LEAST/NOT question, you're looking for a wrong answer—so an extreme answer would be a good choice. Try one:

> With which of the following statements would a scientist most likely DISAGREE?
>
> (A) Although using scientific method can be tedious and time-consuming, it helps scientists accumulate useful data.
> (B) Some scientific breakthroughs, such as genetic engineering, should be used carefully so as not to cause harm.
> (C) A good scientist tries to be objective, remaining skeptical of her own assumptions.
> (D) Science can be used to further the interests of mankind.
> (E) Scientific inquiry always produces evidence that will prove or disprove a scientific hypothesis.

Science Bonus Round

If I'm a researcher testing the effects of a new flea shampoo for dogs, what's the best choice for my control group?

(A) a group of unshampooed cats

(B) a group of unshampooed poodles

(C) a group of men with fleas

Answer to Science Bonus Round

(B) a group of unshampooed poodles

If I'm testing the effect of something on dogs, my control group should consist of dogs, too.

Here's how to crack it

Which answer is the most extreme? The most difficult to prove? That would be (E), which claims that scientific inquiry *always* gets results. No scientist would agree with that—they're naturally suspicious of such absolute statements, because of their subjectivity.

Remember to use POE, and look for the flaws in the answers; when you're doing an EXCEPT question, you shouldn't find any flaws in four of them. The remaining one will be the correct answer.

SUMMARY

1. Review the list of terms. Concentrate on biology, since about half the questions on the Science section will be on biology.

2. Use your common sense. Some answers will violate common sense, and you can eliminate them. For example, *Scientists will eventually learn the answers to every scientific mystery by rigorously using the scientific method.* Or, *Anyone caught littering should be fined heavily and forced to serve jail time.* Such answers are too extreme and silly to be correct, no matter what the question is.

3. Cross out answer that use extreme, absolute answers. When words such as *every* and *always* show up in an answer, it's wrong about 95 percent of the time.

4. Look with favor on answer choices that use mild, weak language, such as *might* or *often*. These answers are harder to disprove than extreme answers, so they're more likely to be right.

5. Finally, don't panic if you see a question asking about something you've never heard of. Your General Knowledge score includes three other sections, for a total of 120 questions. So missing a couple of hard science questions won't matter much at all.

PART ◆ IV

How to Crack the
Test of Communication Skills

10
Listening

HELLO? HELLO?

Yes, that's right, there's a Listening Section. If you've ever taken a standardized test in a foreign language, you've been down this road before. If not, don't worry—taking the section in our diagnostic test is all the practice you need. All you have to do is stay awake, pay attention, and you should do very well.

WHAT DO I NEED TO KNOW?

Nothing. That's the beauty of the Listening Section—you don't have to review anything or learn anything new, because the questions give you all the information you need. The only preparation you need for this section is familiarity with the way it works and a couple of Q-tips for cleaning out your ears.

> ### STATS—LISTENING SECTION
>
> Number of questions: 40
>
> Order of difficulty: yes
>
> Question types: one-sentence statements or questions (20 questions)
>
> Short conversations (11 questions)
>
> Short talks (9 questions)
>
> Techniques: Take light notes, especially if numbers are involved POE
>
> Bubbling: Bubble in each answer as you go along, including guesses

HOW TO CRACK THE LISTENING SECTION

It's true that the Listening Section is easy—if you approach it the right way. It's also easy to make a total mess of it, because you're under pressure to answer each question in the amount of time allotted. You have less control than in other sections, and that can play with your mind. So let's cover a few potential problem spots, so you'll be all set on test day.

- One of the voices has a fairly strong accent. Don't let this rattle you—the accent (probably Spanish) will not be so strong that you can't understand what the person is saying. It just takes a little more concentration.

- Some questions may ask about details. The solution for this is simple—take notes. Don't try to write down every word that is said or even close to it. But if statistics, numbers, times, or days of the week are mentioned, make a quick note of it right on your test booklet.

◆ You must bubble as you go along. Unlike the other sections, in which you should complete a page of questions before bubbling, in the Listening Section you won't have time to go back. That means you have to bubble each question as soon as you can—and if you don't know the answer, go ahead and bubble in your guess before the next question begins. (You will have about 20 seconds in between parts, so if you've left anything blank you can fill it in then.) The biggest threat to your Listening Section score is bubbling mistakes. Make sure you practice bubbling when you take the diagnostic test in the back of this book.

◆ You may not be ready when the next question begins. This is the scary thing about the Listening Section. On the other sections, you can spend more time on a question if you need to. You can (and should) reread it if you get confused or lose your concentration. Here, you get about 13 seconds to choose your answer, and that's it. It's very important to accept the fact that you will most likely lose your concentration at some point, and it's equally important not to get freaked out when it does happen. If you start thinking about lunch and miss an entire question, don't sweat it—just guess and get ready for the next question. Trouble arises if you panic! Don't try to work on any question other than the one on the tape at that moment.

How to Crack the Question Types

Part A: One-sentence statements or questions

For the first twenty questions, you'll hear only one sentence, either a question or a statement. Then you look in your test booklet and choose the answer that makes the most sense. For a statement, the right answer will agree with the information in the statement. For a question, the right answer will be a direct, clear answer to the question.

The questions in each part are arranged in order of difficulty, so you'll have a chance to warm up on some really easy ones before the longer, more complicated questions come along.

Part B: Short conversations

Next you'll hear six short conversations, each with one to two questions, for a total of eleven questions. Only two people will be talking in any one conversation. Sometimes the speakers will not agree with each other, and you will be asked about the disagreement. You may be asked about the tone of one of the speakers: Does she sound angry, contented, or worried? And again, if anyone mentions anything that you might forget, take a quick note in the margin of your answer booklet.

Good Speaker System

It helps to write "1" just before the conversation begins, so you're ready to make any notes for speaker 1. Follow that with "2" when speaker 2 begins.

Part C: Short talks

Next you'll hear three short talks, which will last anywhere from less than a minute to two minutes. Each talk will have three questions. You might think this section will be the most difficult, since there's more to listen to—but it's probably the easiest, because it's a lot like sitting in class listening to a teacher. Just relax and take a few notes, just like you've done a hundred times before. Listen for the main idea of the talk, and if the speaker mentions anybody who disagrees with him, make a note of it.

SUMMARY

1. Stay calm, even if you don't know an answer. Use Process of Elimination, take a quick guess, and get ready for the next question.

2. Take notes. Don't try to transcribe entire questions—but write down dates, times, numbers, and anything else you might have trouble remembering.

3. Bubble question by question. Don't bother circling answers in your test booklet, because you won't be able to come back to anything. Arrange your test booklet and answer sheet on your desk so that it's easy to shift from one to the other.

4. Remember that you don't have to be perfect. If you miss one question, it's only one question. But if you let a missed question mess up your composure, your bubbling, and the questions that follow, then you've got a real disaster on your hands.

11
Reading

I'M TIRED JUST THINKING ABOUT IT

We don't blame you. The NTE is a really long test, and reading 15 passages takes a lot of concentration. Luckily, none of the passages are very long, and you don't have to rely on either your memory or your powers of deduction to get the answers right.

HOW COME?

The great thing about the Reading section is that the correct answer is right there in the passage. Your job is simply to find it. Keep in mind that reading on a standardized test is very different from any other kind of reading—especially the reading you've done in school. You will have to read more closely, but you will not have to think critically or draw conclusions. In fact, you should never draw conclusions yourself! If the question asks for a conclusion, look in the passage to find it.

YOU MEAN I'M NOT SUPPOSED TO THINK?

That's right. A majority of the questions ask you to do nothing more than restate what's in the passage. If you think too much and drag in your own thoughts and feelings about the passage, you're likely to get the answer wrong. The hardest thing about this section is that it takes some concentration, stamina, and the ability to remain objective.

STATS—READING SECTION

Number of questions: 30

Percentage of fact-based questions: 0%

Order of difficulty: yes

Question types: around 13 short passages or statements followed by 1–3 questions each; around 2 longer passages with 5 or 6 questions each

Techniques: POE; scope; reading the question first

Bubbling: page by page; in the final 5 minutes, switch to one question at a time

---

How to Crack the Passages

1. Before reading the passage, jump down and read the question first. Why is this helpful? Simply because if the question asks for the author's main point, you can have that in mind while you read the passage, and you'll get the right answer faster and more accurately. Your reading will be more focused, and you won't waste time worrying about irrelevant parts of the passage.

2. Next, read the passage at about medium speed—don't rush, but don't try to memorize every word. You can always go back to the passage for anything you don't remember. One of the things that causes test takers anxiety during the Reading section is that they feel a lot of pressure to absorb the material instantly—but that's impossible, as well as silly, because the passage isn't going to disappear. You should get into the habit of going back to the passage often to re-read relevant sentences. You'll probably lose your concentration more than once during this section, but it's no reason to panic. It won't be a problem if you simply go back and re-read to get back on track.

3. Re-read the question. If the passage had any length at all, you may not remember the question exactly—and the answer choices may include statements that are true but don't answer the question correctly. It's easy to fall for them if you aren't precisely sure what's being asked.

4. Answer the question in your head (unless it's an inference question). Consider the answer choices to be dangerous temptations. If you look at them too soon—maybe even thinking they'll help you understand the passage better—you're likely to get lured into picking the wrong answer.

5. Now you're all set. You've read the passage and the question, and you've got a good idea of what the right answer will look like. Now go to the answer choices and use Process of Elimination. Be brutal here—if the answer has only one thing wrong with it, cross it out.

6. You don't have to spend time working on every question. The passages and question get somewhat more difficult as you go along, and you are under time pressure. So keep a moderate pace. If you don't finish, that's fine—just remember to fill in your chosen letter on your answer sheet for any questions you don't get to. It doesn't help your score if you rush through the easier stuff to get to harder stuff. If you hit a passage that you can't seem to focus on, skip it, guess, and do the next one.

Reading's an Open Book

Think of the Reading section as an open-book test—the answers are right there in front of you, and all you have to do is look them up in the passage.

Let's try one:

> Students at Fluvanna County high schools have petitioned their school board to change the county-wide grading system, claiming that it is much tougher than the one used in neighboring counties. It is true that a Fluvanna high school student will fail with a grade of 74, while students in nearby counties will pass with a grade of 65 or higher. Yet the difference in grading systems really has no effect, because teachers do not score tests in the same way, and so the percentage of students earning failing grades is no higher in Fluvanna County than in neighboring counties.

The author's main point is best described by which of the following?

Now before you sneak a look at the choices, answer the question first. What is the author getting at? Which of the sentences is more opinion than fact? Right—the final sentence. So the main point is something like "difference in grading systems doesn't matter." You don't have to form your answer into perfect English—you just want a quick phrase that sums it up.

Now for the answers. Don't look for the right answer. Instead, look for anything that's wrong, and cross it out.

(A) To correct unfairness, high school students should be graded on an equal basis.

(B) Fluvanna County school officials believe that a stricter grading system benefits students in the long run.

(C) Grading systems are unimportant when compared with the failure of many students to gain basic skills.

(D) Fluvanna County students are not at a disadvantage due to the stricter grading system used by other counties' schools.

(E) Fluvanna County students should be able to pass with a grade of 65 or higher.

Here's how to crack it

Remember, you're not looking for the best answer—you're looking for any reason to eliminate an answer. Choice (A) is incorrect because the author doesn't believe unfairness exists, and he makes no recommendation for taking any kind of action. Why would anyone choose answer (A)? Because it seems like such a reasonable statement, and because maybe it's what the test taker herself believes should happen. Never choose an answer because you agree with it—you should only be thinking about what agrees with the passage!

Choice (B) is incorrect because there is no mention in the passage of why Fluvanna County has a strict grading system. Again, people will choose this answer if they are looking for something that seems reasonable or likely, but that

---

What *Not* To Do

- Don't spend a long time reading the passage, trying to memorize every word.
- Don't ponder the information in the passage, figuring out how you feel about it.
- Don't spend a long time on a passage that's giving you trouble, because you insist on doing the questions in order.

is not your job on reading questions. You are only interested in what the passage actually says.

Choice (C) is incorrect for the same reason—if the author never talks about "basic skills," then you shouldn't pick an answer that does. Notice that this answer starts off pretty well; the author does think that in the case of Fluvanna County, grading systems are unimportant. Make sure you read the entire answer before picking it. Read answer choices carefully until you find a reason to eliminate it. (Once you find something wrong with an answer choice, stop reading, cross it out, and move on.)

Choice (D) is correct. It restates the author's main point, which is that the tougher grading system in Fluvanna County isn't hurting the students there. If that answer didn't jump out you, don't worry, as long as you didn't find a reason to eliminate it. If you can't decide whether to eliminate an answer, leave it in. Maybe you'll eliminate the rest of them and that will be that.

Choice (E) is incorrect because it is the opposite of what the author says. He does not favor changing the grading system of Fluvanna County, because he doesn't think it makes any difference.

How to Crack the Answer Choices

You'll be using POE whenever you deal with the answer choices in the Reading section, but how do you eliminate? Essentially, in three ways:

1. Scope

An answer choice is out of scope if it contains something that was not mentioned in the passage. In the example about the Fluvanna County students, answer choices (B) and (C) were out of scope because they contained the phrases "benefits students in the long run" and "gain basic skills," neither of which were mentioned in the passage. Scope is very useful for all types of questions—if you spot even a small part of an answer choice that is out of scope, eliminate it and move on.

2. Bad inference

If an answer choice sticks to the subject but makes a big, unwarranted assumption, it will be incorrect no matter how reasonable the assumption may seem. In our example, choice (A) was a bad inference (as well as contradictory to the author). While it did not stray from the subject of the passage, it went too far. If you have a choice between an answer that almost exactly repeats what the passage says, and one that is a little broader or takes the information a little further, go with the former.

3. Stuck?

Sometimes you'll do everything right and still get stuck with two answers you can't decide between. Here's what to do: First, re-read the question. You may have slightly forgotten the exact wording. Next, re-read anything in the passage that's relevant—go ahead and re-read the whole thing if it's short. Are either of your remaining answers out of scope? Last, compare the answers closely. How are they different? Focus on those differences, and decide which one is worse. Part of the reason people get stuck between two answers is that they start trying

Reading Quiz #1

Which of the following is out of scope for the Bad Inference paragraph?
(A) subject matter of a passage
(B) wild assumptions
(C) deductive reasoning

Answer to Reading Quiz #1

(C) deductive reasoning
It's not mentioned in the paragraph, is it?

to figure out which one is better. That's a mistake. During the pressure of the test, you can easily convince yourself that a wrong answer is right—so avoid that trap by scrutinizing the answers for things that make them wrong.

HOW TO CRACK THE QUESTION TYPES

You don't want to answer all reading questions the same way. The particular technique depends on the type of question. As you practice, analyze your mistakes. Do you tend to make mistakes on the same type of question? Then re-read the following tips to figure out exactly what you're doing wrong.

1. Main idea

Approximate number per section: 7
Examples:

> The main idea of the passage is that . . .
> The author's primary purpose is to . . .
> Which of the following best summarizes the main idea of this statement?
> Which of the following statements best expresses the author's main point in the passage?
> The author asserts which of the following?

Here's how to crack it

These questions, like the one you just did, ask you to sum up the author's point. Make sure you figure that out by reading the passage and stopping to think about it before looking at the answer choices. State the main point in your head. Then go to the answers and use POE. With your pencil, cross out answers that are out of scope or make bad inferences.

2. Specific

Approximate number per section: 10
Examples:

> The passage supplies information that would answer which of the following questions?
> The author mentions the land use agreement in order to show that . . .
> According to the passage, some teachers believe the introduction of computers into the classroom can cause which of the following problems?
> The author's description of home schooling informs us of which of the following?

Here's how to crack it

If the question is short, like the last example above, focus on the thing or idea mentioned in the question—in this case, home schooling. When you read the passage, pay close attention to any part that talks about that thing or idea. Reread the question. Answer the question in your head. Then go to the answers and use POE.

If the question is long and confusing, don't spend a lot of time trying to untangle it. Go ahead and read the passage, then read the question, and go back to the passage to find the answer.

The two most important things you can do to get a specific question right are to stick exactly with the information given and to go back to the passage if you have the slightest doubt about the answer. Don't rely on your memory! You should always get specific questions right—the information is explicitly stated in the passage, and all you have to do is find it and spit it back. There is absolutely no thinking, reasoning, or deducing involved.

3. Roman numeral

Approximate number per section: 4

Roman numeral questions usually ask about specific details from the passage. Use the usual technique for answering specific questions. The only difference comes in handling the Roman numerals. After the passage and the question, you will be given three groups that look like this:

I.   The best time of day for learning
II. The most effective way to memorize data
III. An alternative method for taking notes

Quick Time Tip

If you're jammed for time, consider doing Inference questions on your second or even third pass.

Here's how to crack it

Do them one Roman numeral at a time, starting with whichever one seems easiest at first glance. Let's say you start with II. Decide whether it is right or wrong. (Of course, look back to the passage if you have any doubt.) If it's right, check it off and jump to the answer choices, crossing out every answer choice that doesn't include II. If it's wrong, cross out every answer choice that does include II. Proceed to either I or III. If at any point you've crossed out all but one answer, pick it and go on to the next question. All you're doing is applying POE to this particular question format.

If you're running short of time, you may want to skip Roman numeral questions, because they take longer to do.

4. Inference

Approximate number per section: 5

Examples:

Which of the following can be inferred from the results of the study described above?
The author implies that which of the following would have resulted if the study had been complete?
Which of the following is the most accurate inference from the statements above?

Here's how to crack it

Inference questions are slightly more difficult than the other kinds; you will find more of them toward the end of the section. Don't assume that because you're being asked for an inference that you should start thinking broadly about the topic of the passage. Your job is still the same: Cross out anything that strays even slightly from what is in the passage. Only pick an answer that has to be true given the information in the passage. Avoid picking answers that you think are true based on your own knowledge, or that you personally agree with.

SUMMARY

1. Read the question first.

2. Read the passage, focusing on the information relevant to the question.

3. Re-read the question.

4. For all but inference questions, answer the question in your head before looking at the answer choices.

5. Use POE. Eliminate answers that are out of scope or bad inferences. Don't pick answers just because you agree with them.

6. Always look for the flaws in the answer choices rather than for the answer that seems right or most logical. Stick with the information in the passage.

7. Don't go too fast. Don't feel you have to spend time on all the questions—but try to be thorough and correct on the ones you do spend time on.

12

Writing

First, the Bad News

If you never had grammar in school, you're going to have to learn some now. Although this section is not horribly difficult, you can't simply depend on your ear to lead you to the correct answers.

What's Wrong with My Ear?

Well, nothing—except that it probably isn't perfect at identifying standard written English. Most of us violate quite a few rules of grammar when we speak, and so we're used to the way incorrect grammar sounds.

On the other hand, if you've read a lot of good books, your ear is probably pretty well trained. Reading good writing trains your ear better than anything else. How can you tell how good your ear is? If you overlook mistakes because they sound fine to you, then don't trust your ear. Learn the grammar errors covered in this chapter and use the checklist when doing test questions.

One more bit of bad news: Multiple-choice writing has more questions than any other section, so you have to work relatively quickly if you want to take a good look at all the questions.

Ready for the Good News?

You don't need to know every little niggling detail of English grammar to do well. Some common grammar mistakes show up frequently, so don't try to memorize an entire grammar textbook. Instead, focus on the errors reviewed in this chapter. The number of things you need to learn is finite and manageable; you can expect to improve on this section if you study and practice.

More good news: Process of elimination works great! Go back and review Basic and Advanced Principles in chapters 3 and 4. Make sure you aren't slipping back into the old bad habit of looking for the right answer instead of eliminating wrong answers.

STATS—WRITING SECTION

Number of questions: 45

Order of difficulty: yes

Question types: Usage: find the underlined error in the sentence, if there is one (25 questions)

Sentence correction: choose the correct version of the sentence (10 questions)

Composition: answer questions about editing a passage (10 questions)

Techniques: POE

Extra review: *Harbrace College Handbook* (Harcourt, Brace, and World)

QUICK REVIEW: GRAMMAR

PRONOUNS

A pronoun is simply a word that stands in for a noun. On the NTE, a pronoun often refers to a person.

After "No Error," pronoun questions come up more often than any other type, so study them extra carefully. The pronouns you will be tested on most often are:

Subject Pronouns		Object Pronouns		Possessive Pronouns	
(sing.)	(plural)	(sing.)	(plural)	(sing.)	(plural)
I	we	me	us	my	our
you	you	you	you	your	your
he/she	they	him/her	them	his/her	their
it		it		its	
who	who	whom	whom	whose	whose

Singular pronouns: this, that, each, another, other
Plural pronouns: those, these, some, both

Subject pronouns are used as the subject of a sentence: *I* flew out of the window.

Object pronouns are used as the object of a verb, preposition, or infinitive. In other words, object pronouns are NOT the subject of a sentence and do not perform an action: Mary tickled *me* with a feather.

Possessive pronouns simply show ownership: It's *my* sweatshirt; *his* bathtub; that ugly lamp is *yours*.

Pronoun agreement

> **Rule:** A pronoun must agree in number and gender with the noun it stands for.

What this means is that if the pronoun stands for a singular thing, the pronoun must be singular as well. Singular goes with singular and plural goes with plural; feminine goes with feminine and masculine goes with masculine.

Correct: The girls took off their boots and threw them at their teacher.

Wrong: The girls took off her boots and threw it at her teacher.

Wrong: The girls took off they're boots and threw them at their teacher.

The boots belong to the girls, so the correct possessive pronoun is the plural *their*. The boots are plural too, so the correct pronoun is *them*. Notice that the boots aren't performing any action, so the pronoun is an object pronoun.

Run to the Nearest Bookstore

Get a copy of *Grammar Smart*, by the staff of The Princeton Review. It offers even more detail on all the grammar you need to know (and we promise it's not boring).

In the last example, notice that *they're* is the contraction of *they are*; don't confuse it with *their*. (Or *there*. Don't you love homophones?)

As for the gender part of the rule, you know this already—use *he/him/his* for males and *she/her/hers* for females. And be glad you're not studying French, in which every noun has a gender.

Antecedents

> **Rule:** A pronoun should always have a clear antecedent.

What's an antecedent? The word that the pronoun refers to. In the example sentence above about the girls and their boots, the antecedent for *them* is *boots*.

Correct: Mabel and Eunice walked around the block twice before they went inside.

or: Mabel and Eunice walked around the block twice before Mabel went inside.

Wrong: Mabel and Eunice walked around the block twice before she went inside.

In the incorrect example, the antecedent for *she* could be either Mabel or Eunice—it's ambiguous. So it's wrong.

Here's how to crack it

Run through a checklist. First, check the antecedent. If that's clear, check to see if the number of the pronoun matches that of its antecedent.

Remember that if you find something wrong, that's the answer.

QUICK QUIZ—PRONOUNS

Correct the pronoun problems, if any, in the following sentences. (There may be more than one problem, and you may have to make some other alterations in the sentence when you fix the pronouns.) The answers are on page 100.

1. The head of the English department posted those who had passed the oral examination on the department bulletin board, and even sent them notes of congratulation.

2. Its never a good idea to adopt a stray cat without taking them to a veterinarian first.

3. The company president and the chief financial officer got on the elevator without remembering to take his briefcase, and so he had to run back to get it before the meeting could begin.

4. Taking him at his word, the lawyer, who had just passed the bar, began to prepare his defense, although she was not aware of many facts of his case.

Quick Pronoun Tip

Every time you see a pronoun underlined, ask yourself:
- What is the antecedent? Is it clear?
- Does the pronoun agree in number with its antecedent?
- Is there any confusion about whether the pronoun is possessive or a contraction? (Think of *its* versus *it's*.)

---

5. There are several reasons why they should consult they're records before submitting their tax returns; if they aren't careful, they're going to be audited and lose their savings.

VERBS

A verb is an action word, such as *run, screamed,* or *will be sneezing.* If a verb is underlined, you need to check only two things: agreement and tense.

Agreement

> **Rule:** The subject and verb must agree in number.

Same deal as for pronouns: Singular subjects take singular verbs, and plural subjects take plural verbs. If you wouldn't know a plural verb if you woke up next to one, don't worry; you're like most people. All you have to do is locate the subject, and you'll probably be able to tell if the verb is correct by ear.

Correct the following:

> Loreen and Nate, carrying a big box, is on the
> way to the Salvation Army.

What's the verb? *is.*

What's the subject of the verb? In other words, who or what is on the way? *Loreen and Nate.*

Does *Loreen and Nate is* sound right to you? We hope not. The sentence should read:

> Loreen and Nate, carrying a big box, are on
> the way to the Salvation Army.

What's a little tricky about that sentence is that *box* comes right before *is,* and if *box* were the subject of the verb, then *is* would be correct. So your ear could be fooled.

Here's how to crack it

If a verb is underlined, find its subject by asking who or what is doing the action. Then see if the verb and subject agree, paying close attention to singular and plural.

Tense

We use different verb tenses to show when something happened. For instance, I *will do* the laundry means I haven't done it yet, so *will do* is in the future tense. But you don't need to know the names of tenses for the NTE. Just avoid a few common tense errors and be careful when the sentence is long.

Correct the following:

> If we would have played our usual number,
> we would have won the lottery.

The problem here is that the *would* tense is used twice. Simplify by using the *had* tense instead:

> If we had played our usual number, we
> would have won the lottery.

The correction makes more sense, because playing the number happens before winning the lottery, and now the tenses make that clear.

Correct the following:

> After she practices the tuba for a month, Junie
> was able to play one song.

Confusing to read, isn't it? That's because the sentence jumps from the present tense to the past tense, mixing up the order of what happened. She practiced before she learned the song, right? So the sentence should read:

> After she practices the tuba for a month, Junie
> will be able to play one song.

You have to pay attention to all the clues in the sentence—the *after* is crucial in making clear what happened when.

Here's how to crack it

Stay alert for words that indicate time, such as *before, during, after, later*, and *while*. Occasionally, dates might be important as well. If the events in the sentence happened in 1910, you'll be using a past tense.

Parallel construction

Rule: Verbs in a list should be in the same form.

Correct the following:

> Daquan brushed his teeth, washed his face,
> and climbs into bed.

The list is *brushed, washed*, and *climbs*—the last verb is not in the same tense as the first two. The sentence should read:

> Daquan brushed his teeth, washed his face,
> and climbed into bed.

Here's how to crack it

Be on the lookout for lists of verbs like the one above, and make sure everything on the list is consistent.

The rule of parallel construction applies to phrases, too:

Correct: Let's go to the shoe store, to the market, and to the skating rink.

Wrong: Let's go to the shoe store, the market, and to the skating rink.

In the incorrect example, the *to* is dropped in the second phrase and then pops up again in the third. That's inconsistent, and it violates the rule. (Note: You could also correctly write *to the shoe store, the market, and the skating rink*. The *to* is understood to control the phrases that follow.)

On the NTE, parallel construction errors will most often involve verbs.

QUICK QUIZ—VERBS

Correct the verb errors in the following sentences, if there are any. The answers are on page 102.

1. Before she thought about running for office, she should figure out how her platform differs from that of the current councilman.

2. If the sun were to explode, it would take many minutes before the effects of the explosion were felt on Earth.

3. Having been to the beach many times before, the children were unafraid of the crashing surf and raced up and down the dunes, splashed in the water, and were building an enormous sand castle.

4. The trash collector, as well as the nurses, were deciding whether to go on strike when the nursing home manager announced salary cuts.

5. To the surprise of scientists researching global warming, a certain kind of flea has been proven to produce much more methane gas than do cows, who are previously being blamed for the dangerously high levels of methane that are damaging the ozone layer.

IDIOMS

An idiom is a kind of exception, a rule unto itself. For instance, we say:

Wow, I am really spaced out.

Not

Wow, I am really spaced off.

You'll generally be tested on which preposition to use for a particular idiom, which is not as bad as it sounds, because you probably use idioms correctly without thinking about it.

But when you're doing sentence correction questions, you may be faced with four wrong idioms, and it's easy to get confused. The best way to study them is to look over the following list from time to time. Better yet, make your own list and keep it in your pocket and add to it when you discover new ones while reading the newspaper or watching a movie. You can study the list when you're waiting for the bus, in the line at the bank, or whenever you have a spare couple of minutes.

Quick Verb Tip

Every time you see a verb underlined, ask yourself:

- What is the subject of the verb? Do the subject and verb sound right together?
- Does the tense of the verb make sense?
- Are the verbs part of a list? If so, are they all in the same form?

comply with: You must comply with the rules.

prior to: Prior to voting, you must register.

preferable to: Your spaghetti sauce is preferable to mine.

superior to: My nachos are superior to yours.

try to: We decided to try to earn money selling potholders. (incorrect: try and)

prohibit from: Small children should be prohibited from drinking whiskey.

define as: Some people define happiness as working hard and playing hard.

different from: You are no different from me. (incorrect: different than)

intend to: I intend to keep eating mushrooms. (incorrect: intend on)

between x and y: I can't decide between this dress and that one. (incorrect: between x or y)

PASSIVE AND ACTIVE VOICE

This one is a pet peeve of ours, mostly because voice errors are so rampant—you can read them almost anywhere, even though they are a sure sign of bad writing.
Which sounds better to you:

> The presidency was resigned by Richard Nixon today.

> Richard Nixon resigned as president today.

Doesn't the second example seem stronger and more concise? That's because it's an example of active voice: Richard Nixon resigned. The subject of the sentence actively does something.

The first example flips parts of the sentence around, making the presidency the subject of the verb instead of Richard Nixon. This is passive voice, a much weaker form of expression.

> **Rule:** Use active voice, not passive.

Voice errors are much more likely to appear during the second (sentence correction) part of the section than during the first (usage) part.

OTHER DETAILS

Some errors show up only once or twice per test, if that. And you may find some of these errors easy to spot. But in the interest of thoroughness, keep an eye out for:

Redundancy

Redundancy is saying the same thing twice. In other words, it's wordy.

> **Rule:** Avoid redundancy and wordiness.

Examples:

small in size

circulate around

annually each year

consensus of opinion

reason . . . is because

collaborate together

All of these phrases are wordy and are a mark of bad writing. Redundant phrases may appear in the first part of the section; however, you will probably have to correct wordiness in the second and third parts. On the second part (sentence correction), if two choices have the same meaning but one is longer and more roundabout, choose the shorter one.

Diction

Good diction is using words correctly. If you say, "That tornado was incredulous!" you're guilty of a diction error—you meant incredible, not incredulous.

> **Rule:** Use good diction.

Other pairs of commonly confused words:

allusion and illusion

complement and compliment

former and latter

principle and principal

If you come across an underlined word you don't know, don't assume it's a diction error. But if only one word is underlined, make sure it's a word that fits in that context.

Adjective/Adverb

This type of error may show up once or twice per section. People usually miss this error because they are reading the questions too quickly.

> **Rule:** Adjectives modify nouns. Adverbs modify verbs, adjectives, or other adverbs.

You don't need to get too deep into this—just be on the lookout for a word that's missing the -ly on the end. Example:

incorrect: She ran as quick as she could.

correct: She ran as quickly as she could.

Like/As

This pair tends to make people nervous. But you can relax; the errors on the NTE will usually be pretty glaring, and there won't be many of them.

> **Rule:** *Like* is used to compare nouns (people, places, things).

Examples:

correct: Like Bob, I appreciate a good burrito.

incorrect: As does Bob, I appreciate a good burrito.

Remember:

First Pass: easy questions.
Second Pass: questions you
kinda-sorta know.
Third Pass: fill in your pre-
selected answer.

> **Rule:** *As* is used with *such* to make a list.

correct: Mary packed such items as a canteen, some cookies, and cat food.

incorrect: Mary packed such items like a canteen, some cookies, and cat food.

Punctuation

Not a big deal, but commas and semicolons will show up a couple of times in this section.

> **Rule:** A semicolon (;) is used to separate two complete sentences.

Example:

> I ate a box of cookies; I felt so sick I had to stay home.

> **Rule:** Use commas to set off appositives and phrases that are long and not part of the main sentence.

Example:

> Mr. Lardgate, a man with a very big nose, decided to see a plastic surgeon.

In that example, the short description a man with a very big nose is known as an appositive. A different example:

> It is a main concern of all city council members that the budget not only cover basic necessities, such as education, street repairs, and the police department, but also allow for emergencies like snow removal.

Notice how you could yank *such as education, street repairs, and the police department* out of the sentence without turning it into a fragment? Since the phrase is so long, it's better to set it off from the main sentence with commas.

Comma placement, in some circumstances, is a matter of personal choice. ETS test writers don't want to get into a shouting match over commas, so if there is a question on commas, just remember the rules described above.

Capitalization

> **Rule:** Proper nouns should be capitalized.

That includes:

  days of the week

  months of the year

  countries

  continents

  titles of books and plays

  religions

Sentence fragments

> **Rule:** A sentence needs both a subject and a verb to be complete.

Did you ever have a teacher mark "frag" in the margin of one of your essays? Maybe you had written something like this:

> The poet, regarded as a genius with both imagery and meter, although usually her poems did not rhyme.

Whoa there! The sentence starts off well enough with poet as the subject. But where is the verb to go with it? Don't be confused by the clause *although usually her poems did not rhyme*. It can't stand alone as a sentence either, and a bunch of dependent clauses does not a sentence make.

HOW TO CRACK THE QUESTION TYPES

Now that you've finished reviewing, it's time to look at the questions as they'll appear on the NTE. Remember, the goal is not to learn all of English grammar but to get the NTE grammar questions right. So the techniques we'll describe are as important as your knowledge of grammar (as far as this exam is concerned, anyway).

Usage (Part A)

Here's an example:

> The ancient wall drawings <u>are</u> a delight for anthropologists and art
>   A
>
> <u>scholars alike</u>, because <u>it depicts</u> everyday activities for the long-ago culture
>   B   C
>
> and <u>because the artistic techniques are</u> unique. <u>No Error</u>
>   D   E

Here's how to crack it

First, read it through all the way at your normal, everyday reading speed. Does anything jump out at you? If so, try to name the grammatical problem. If you don't see an error, start the checklist. Look for pronouns first. Aha, choice (C)! Ask yourself what the *it* is standing in for. In other words, what *depicts everyday activities*? Right—the *ancient wall drawings*, which is plural. So *it* should be changed to *they*. (Not that you have to worry about the correction. All you have to do is spot the errors.)

Let's say the pronoun had been okay. Check the verbs next. Then check the idioms. If you still can't find anything, pick No Error and move on.

WHAT IF I CAN'T FIND THE ERROR, BUT I KNOW IT'S THERE SOMEWHERE?

Circle the question and come back to it after you've gone through the rest of the questions in that part of the test. (Or you can wait until you've finished the entire section.) It's easy to lose your focus after reading a sentence five times—it all starts to sound meaningless. So keep going and come back later to take another look. A lot of the time the answer will seem obvious. If it doesn't, just take a guess and forget about it. Remember, you aren't supposed to get all of the questions right.

OR MAYBE YOU'RE JUST PARANOID

Since there are five possible answers, you can expect No Error to be the right answer approximately one-fifth of the time. The overwhelming majority of test takers don't pick No Error often enough—you should expect to see around five of them in Part A alone.

WHAT'S WRONG WITH THIS SENTENCE?

Nothing. Of course, an NTE question may be a little more difficult. You may be given a sentence with complicated syntax, lots of pronouns, and plenty of different tenses, such as:

> The men, whose feet were tired after the
> weeks of hiking, were nonetheless prepared
> to keep going until they reached the cave
> where the treasure had been hidden by the
> retreating army.

Error-Free Sentences

Don't be afraid to pick No Error, especially if you've checked the sentence carefully but can't find anything wrong. Make sure you have roughly three to six No Errors in Part A.

Now, ordinarily you might read a sentence like that and think nothing of it, but when you're taking the NTE, it's easy to get paranoid and begin imagining grammar errors all over the place. Everything becomes suspect.

POE Is Still Your Pal

Remember that the process of taking the NTE is not like taking a test in school. The right answer is right there on the page in front of you. Your job is to eliminate the wrong answers and choose what's left.

As you go through your checklist, cross out answers in your test booklet if they pass muster. If the pronoun agrees with its antecedent, cross it out. We know we keep harping on this, but you'll find it much easier to make good guesses on difficult questions if you've visually eliminated the dead wood first.

What About Order of Difficulty?

The questions get harder both within the three parts and in the section as a whole. In other words, people tend to like Part A better than Part B, and Part B better than Part C. And the questions within those parts get harder as you go along.

That means you shouldn't hurry through the beginning of each part. If the questions start to get too hard for you, speed up, guess, and move to the next part.

If, however, you happen to do better on Part B or C, by all means do that part first and come back later for the rest. It's always a good idea to do the questions you feel most confident about first.

Sentence correction (Part B)

Here's an example:

> The townspeople preferred having new bike
> lanes on Main Street rather than to build more
> parking spaces.
>
> (A)   rather than to build
> (B)   than to build
> (C)   to building
> (D)   than building
> (E)   than build

Here's how to crack it

First, read the sentence through—but stop reading if you think something has gone wrong. Did you hesitate when you got to the phrase *to build*? Good for you. Can you tell what's wrong with it? If you think it's a parallelism problem, you'd be right. What did the townspeople prefer? They preferred *having* to *building*. So go to the answer choices and cross out any answer than doesn't use *building*. That gets rid of (A), (B), and (E). Now take a look at the remaining choices. How are they different? (C) uses *to* and (D) uses *than*. Which sounds better to you in the sentence? Choice (C) is correct, because the right idiom is *prefer to*.

HOW'S THAT AGAIN?

Start by reading the question. The second you hit something that sounds off, stop reading. Try to identify the error. Go to the answer choices and cross out anything that doesn't correct that specific error. Then inspect the remaining choices for differences and continue to eliminate.

SHOULDN'T I JUST LOOK FOR THE RIGHT ANSWER?

Absolutely not. The right answer is buried among four wrong choices, which makes it hard to distinguish. Reading wrong choices that are full of bad grammar tends to throw off even the best of us. You'll get a higher score by focusing on the ways the answer choices differ, and eliminating the ones with errors. Whatever is left is your answer.

WHAT IF I GET STUCK?

First, circle the number in your answer booklet so you can come back to it if you have time. Then take a guess. Choose the simplest, clearest, shortest answer. More complicated answer choices are less likely to be correct.

Part C: Composition

This is a relatively new question type, a kind of hybrid of reading composition and grammar. You'll most likely be asked about the organization of a short passage, about the appropriate use of some linking words such as *however* and *nonetheless*, and about the author's tone or attitude. This part looks worse than it is—and it's only ten questions long. You should spend the least amount of time on this part of the writing section.

First, a short list of terms that are often used in Composition questions:

metaphor: a comparison. If you call your boyfriend "Honey," you're not suggesting he really is honey, you're saying he is sweet and tasty like honey. (See? Metaphors pop up in places other than English class!) On Part C, you may be asked to identify a metaphor, or to choose an answer that continues a metaphor already begun in the passage.

fact: something that is generally agreed to be true, such as "The Earth is round" or "Thomas Jefferson died on July 4th." A fact may be disputed by a nut or two (like those who insist the Holocaust never happened), but if the statement is accepted as fact by most of the world, consider it a fact.

opinion: any statement influenced by the thoughts, feelings, or personal experience of the writer or speaker. Look for words of evaluation such as *best, favorite, unpleasant,* or *stupid.* Agreeing with an opinion does not make it fact. On Part C, you will probably be asked to distinguish between fact and opinion.

tone: the manner or style of a piece of writing or speech; its attitude. For example, *I hate your guts* is written in an angry tone, and *Frankly, my dear, I don't give a damn* was spoken in a condescending tone. If you're asked about the tone of a passage, it's best to read the passage over and think about it before you look at the answer choices; otherwise, you may allow the answer choices to sway your judgment.

flow: the smoothness of a piece of writing. You'll probably be asked to pick out which sentence in a short passage interrupts the flow. It's the sentence that stands out when you read it—the one that seemed sudden, strange, and out of place.

Here's an example:

(1) According to polls done both by government agencies and by airline companies themselves, the public generally accepts airplane travel as safe. (2) After all, many thousands more people are killed each year in automobiles than in planes. (3) _____ whenever a large plane crashes and receives attention in the national media, confidence in the airlines plummets, even if the crash is the first one to occur in years. (4) Also, government safety efforts have focused much more intensely on drivers and highways than on airline regulation, perhaps partly in reaction to the public assumption of airline safety. (5) One might draw the conclusion that the public's feelings of safety are largely affected by the media, rather than by statistics or even personal experience.

1. Which transitional adverb is appropriate to complete sentence (3)?

(A) Yet
(B) Moreover
(C) Therefore
(D) Consequently
(E) Besides

Here's how to crack it

First of all, forget the term *transitional adverb.* Just substitute *word* for it, and move ahead to answer the question. (No one asked you to define or identify a transitional adverb, right? So don't decide in advance that you can't answer the question correctly.) If the public thinks planes are safe but get worried when they see a plane crash on the evening news, you have a reverse in direction—not worried to suddenly worried. Therefore, you need a word that expresses that change in direction. *However* would do it, but it's not one of the choices. Just read sentence (2), substitute in an answer choice, and read sentence (3). Eliminate the ones that don't make sense. Which one fits best? That's right—(A) Yet.

Try another question on the same passage.

2. The flow of the passage would be improved if which of the following sentences were switched?

(A) 1 and 2
(B) 2 and 3
(C) 3 and 4
(D) 3 and 5
(E) 4 and 5

Here's how to crack it

Did any of the sentences seem awkwardly placed when you first read the passage? We hope you said (4), because it talks about cars, which were mentioned in sentence (2). Why would the author bring up cars, then forget about them, and then bring them up again? Only because the author is disorganized. Eliminate every answer that doesn't include (4)—that's (A), (B), and (D). As for choice (E), sentence (5) talks about a conclusion, so it belongs at the end. The right answer is (C). To check it, read the passage quickly with (3) and (4) switched, and see if it makes better sense. (It does, doesn't it?)

Keep in mind that the passages on Part C will not be distinguished by free-flowing creativity; the sentences should follow each other like footsteps, in an orderly progression.

SUMMARY

1. Make sure you study the grammar errors in the review section and know them cold.

2. On Usage questions (Part A), read the sentence quickly to spot glaring mistakes. If you don't see any, check out the verbs and pronouns first.

3. On Sentence Correction questions (Part B), stop reading the question sentence if you spot an error or if it just sounds off. Compare the answer choices, and use POE.

4. Remember that the sentences in Part A and Part B will be correct as is about 20 percent of the time, so don't under-pick No Error—answer choice (E) in Part (A) and answer choice (A) in Part B.

5. On Composition questions (Part C), learn the list of terms—there's only a handful, most of which you probably already know—and relax. Spend the least amount of time on this part, only because these questions will probably take longer to do.

CHAPTER 12—QUICK QUIZ ANSWERS

Pronouns

Here's how the sentences should look, with the changed parts italicized:

1. The head of the English department posted *the names of those* who had passed the oral examination on the department bulletin board, and even sent them notes of congratulation.

   In the incorrect version, it sounds like the department head posted the actual people on the bulletin board. This error falls under the category of an unclear antecedent, because *those* should refer to *those names*, not *those people*. What could be tricky about this sentence is that you know what the author intended—and so you make a little subconscious correction, assigning the pronoun to its proper antecedent. When you take the test, don't assume the pronouns are correct just because you can figure out what the sentence is supposed to mean—the antecedent has to be both clear *and* in the sentence.

2. *It's* never a good idea to adopt a stray cat before taking *it* to a veterinarian first. Or: *It's* never a good idea to adopt stray *cats* before taking *them* to a veterinarian first.

    First of all, *its* is always a possessive pronoun. *It's* is the contraction for *it is*. If you aren't sure which to use, try substituting *it is* for the pronoun—if the substitution makes sense, use *it's*. If it doesn't, use *its*. As for the second problem, *stray cat* is singular, so use *it* instead of *them*. (An animal is correctly referred to as an it.) Or if you like, you can make *cat* plural and keep the plural pronoun *them*.

    On the NTE, you won't have this kind of choice. For example, in this sentence, either the pronoun *them* will be underlined, or *cat*. You don't have to worry about the various options in making a correction.

3. The company president and the chief financial officer got on the elevator without remembering to take *the president's* briefcase, and so *the president* had to run back to get it before the meeting could begin.

    Sure, the sentence is a little awkward—but at least you know whose briefcase it is and who ran back to get it. You could correct this sentence any number of ways, as long as you get rid of the ambiguous *his* and *he*. (If we knew that the company president was female, the pronouns would be OK, because the *he* would have to refer to the financial officer.)

4. No error. You can figure out from the sentence that the lawyer is a *she* and the person in trouble is a *he*, so there's no confusion.

5. There are several reasons why they should consult *their* records before submitting their tax returns; if *they* aren't careful, *they're* going to be audited and lose *their* savings.

    In the correct version, you can see *there*, *their*, and *they're* all used the way they're supposed to be. *Their* is always a possessive pronoun; *they're* is the contraction for *they are*. You can use the same trick as for *its/it's*—substitute *they are* and see what happens.

Analysis: Well, how did you do? Remember that the actual NTE questions should be a little easier, since you don't have to come up with correct versions of anything—it's all multiple choice. Look carefully at the questions you got wrong, understand why, and make a note of the specific rules they test. Then come back and review them later.

Verbs

Here are the correct versions:

1. Before she thought about running for office, she *should have figured* out how her platform differs from that of the current councilman. Or: Before she thinks about running for office, she *should figure* out how her platform differs from that of the current councilman.

   The question here is what happens first. The sentence is trying to say that she should have figured out her platform first, and then thought about running for office. The original sentence gets it backwards.

2. No Error. Avoid changing something just because you don't like the sound of it. Try to have a grammatical reason in mind, especially if you tend to get No Error questions wrong.

3. Having been to the beach many times before, the children were unafraid of the crashing surf and raced up and down the dunes, splashed in the water, and *built* an enormous sand castle.

   A parallel construction error. The list of verbs is *raced*, *splashed*, and *built*. All past tense.

4. The trash collector, as well as the nurses, *was* deciding whether to go on strike when the nursing home manager announced salary cuts.

   A tricky agreement question—the subject of the verb is *trash collector*, so the *trash collector was deciding* is correct. The *nurses* aren't included because they are set off from the subject by commas and the phrase *as well as*. Plus, there's no *and* linking them to the subject. The incorrect sentence sounds pretty good, though—because *nurses* is so close to *were deciding*. Remember to check actively for the subjects of verbs instead of depending on your ear.

5. To the surprise of scientists researching global warming, a certain kind of flea has been proven to produce much more methane gas than do cows, who *were* previously being blamed for the dangerously high levels of methane that are damaging the ozone layer.

Whew. A complicated sentence, with a lot of verbs—but the only problem is that cows used to be blamed until it turned out that the fleas were causing all the trouble. The word *previously* is the big tip-off here. If something was happening previously, it can't be happening in the present tense.

13

The Essay

ON TOP OF EVERYTHING ELSE, I HAVE TO WRITE AN ESSAY?

That's right. But you don't have to produce an absolutely perfect piece of writing—the graders do make allowances for the time limitation. All you have to do is demonstrate that you have organized your thoughts about the topic and that you have some minimal writing skills.

What Do You Mean by Minimal?

You aren't expected to deliver a polished essay. You don't have to write like Henry James, or even Jackie Collins. All you have to do is write in complete sentences, as clearly and simply as you can manage. Writing makes a lot of people nervous, especially under pressure, but if you practice a bit, you'll see that a half an hour really is plenty of time for you to come up with something to write about, organize your thoughts on the topic, and write your essay. Just don't have unrealistic expectations, and relax.

Will the Topic Be Difficult?

Not in the least. You won't need any specific or esoteric outside knowledge in order to write the essay—in fact, it's likely that you will only be asked to write about your own experiences. There's no right or wrong way to respond to the topic. The way you express yourself is much more important than the content of your essay.

Are the Graders Mean?

Not particularly. Mostly, they are in a big hurry. They are not going to spend a lot of time poring over your essay—maybe a minute or so—so you need to make your essay look good at a glance. We've got some strategies to help you do just that.

How to Crack the Essay Section

(First 7–10 minutes)

1. Read the topic over a couple of times. A large part—perhaps the largest part—of mastering a standardized test is simply following the directions. Make sure you know exactly what the topic asks for.

2. Think of an appropriate story to tell. You'll most likely need to relate some personal experience, either from the classroom or everyday life. Think your idea all the way through and make sure that it fits the topic. Don't try to second-guess the graders and figure out what they want you to write about, because, frankly, they don't care. Write about whatever is easy for you to write about.

3. Organize what you're going to say. If you're relating a story, do you need to put it in context first? Does your story need any kind of introduction? What's your conclusion going to be? The organization should not be complicated; at most, you'll need an introduction, an example, and a conclusion. And you may not even need an introduction, depending on the format of the writing task.

4. Pay attention to tone. If you're asked to write a letter to a colleague, the tone should be friendlier and less formal than if you're asked to write a general essay. The tone of your writing should match the format of the task.

(Next 18–21 minutes)

5. Write it. Remember that clarity is the most important thing. Tell your story simply, and pace yourself so that you finish your conclusion and have a couple of minutes to read it over.

(Last 2 minutes)

6. Read it over. Check your spelling and punctuation and make sure everything is legible. (If you can't read a word, cross it out neatly and write it out just above.)

TIPS FOR A HIGH ESSAY SCORE

◆ Make the essay as long as you can. We aren't inviting you to ramble, but if you only scratch out a handful of sentences it will look like you choked or didn't have a thought in your head. So choose a story that will take seven or eight sentences to tell and one that you can comment on briefly.

◆ Paragraph correctly. It makes you look organized. Put your introduction, examples, and conclusion all in separate paragraphs. If you're relating a conversation using quotation marks, each person's speech should have its own paragraph.

◆ Vary your sentences' structure and length. You don't have to get too complicated here, but a lot of short sentences in a row will make your essay seem choppy, and too many long sentences will make your thoughts appear less organized.

◆ Avoid throat-clearing. What we mean is jump right into your subject instead of writing about what you're going to write about. *I am going to write my essay about . . .* is a weak opening for an essay.

◆ Avoid babbling. If at some point while you're writing you aren't sure what to say next, stop and think for a bit. While you want your essay to be long, you don't want it to be full of sentences that are vague and empty or that repeat what you've already said.

- Be specific. If you're telling a story, try to make it as vivid as possible by using details. If you're making an argument, give specific reasons for your position rather than broad generalizations.

- Write neatly. If your essay is a big scrawling mess with lots of crossed out lines, the grader is going to be irritated. You do not want to irritate the grader. If you're not known for beautiful penmanship, make sure to practice writing legibly under time pressure.

ESSAY DRILLS

Here are a couple of sample topics to practice on. Sit down with some notebook paper, a pen, and a stopwatch. Give yourself a strict half hour for each one, and don't look at the topics until the clock is running. It would help to show your essays to a friend who has some editing or writing experience. Also, compare your essays to the ones in *The Official Guide*, to see what you need to improve.

ESSAY DRILL #1

As part of a job application, write a short essay describing your primary goal as a teacher and briefly explain how you plan to achieve your goal.

ESSAY DRILL #2

Describe either the best or worst experience of your own education. How would you encourage or prevent the same thing from happening to your students?

PART V

How to Crack the Test of Professional Knowledge

14

Professional Knowledge

NOW WE'RE TALKING!

Finally, of all the NTE Praxis tests, this is the one you should be best prepared for. If you've only taken one education course, even that will be a big help. And so will any teaching experience you've had.

WHAT DOES IT COVER?

It covers a broad range of topics, some of which you'll be more comfortable with than others. (The question totals in parentheses below are from a recent test.)

1. Planning Instruction (12 questions)
    These questions essentially cover three things:
    ◆ What's your instructional goal?
    ◆ What resources are you going to use to accomplish your goal?
    ◆ What kind of activities are appropriate for your students?

You will need to know how to deal with various classroom complications such as gifted students, students from different cultures who speak different languages, and learning-disabled students.

2. Implementing Instruction (23 questions)
    These questions ask about how you actually teach. If you've taught a class before, use the practical knowledge you have gained from the experience. Some typical topics:
    ◆ If you want to stimulate class discussion, what's the best kind of question to ask?
    ◆ If a student's work is deteriorating, what should you do?
    ◆ What are some ways to teach a child with an impairment (visual, verbal, etc.)?
    ◆ What are the appropriate uses for the various modes of teaching—group instruction, individual instruction, small study groups, etc.?

3. Evaluating Instruction (16 questions)
    These questions are essentially about testing. You'll need to know:
    ◆ The names of different types of tests (cloze, norm-referenced, criterion-referenced), what they are, and when to use them
    ◆ When standardized tests are useful and appropriate
    ◆ How to test students of different cultures and languages
    ◆ How to interpret testing results

4. Managing Instructional Environments (19 questions)
    The education field just loves jargon, doesn't it? "Instructional Environments" just means "the classroom." Again, use your teaching experience to guide you. You'll need to know:
    ◆ How to set limits
    ◆ How to communicate what kind of behavior is acceptable and what is not acceptable

- What to do if a student acts out
- How to promote self-esteem in your students
- How to make your classroom a positive place
- How to recognize inappropriate teaching strategies

5. Professional Foundations (23 questions)
   These questions tend to be the most fact-based; you'll either
   know them or you won't, depending on whether you've taken
   the relevant courses. You'll need to know:
   - Laws pertaining to teachers, disabled students, and schools
   - How economic, social, and cultural factors influence education
   - Developments in education theory
   - The stages in human development (particularly Piaget's stages of cognitive development)

6. Professional Functions (12 questions)
   These questions are about how a teacher should act outside of
   the classroom. You'll need to know:
   - How to deal with parents
   - How to deal with other teachers and school administrators
   - How to deal with community members (special-interest groups, etc.)
   - When to consult a professional organization
   - What kinds of political work are appropriate and what kinds aren't

Great Old Movies About Teachers

Goodbye, Mr. Chips (he's crusty, he's cool, he doesn't bake cookies).
The Prime of Miss Jean Brodie (Maggie Smith is *always* fabulous).
To Sir With Love (plus you get to hear Lulu's hit song).

QUICK REVIEW

Certain terms and vocabulary will show up on the Professional Knowledge section—some that you may not have covered in class. Study this list and you'll be way ahead of the game. Though you probably won't know the answers to at least some of the questions, you can still get a good score.

affective domain: from Bloom's Taxonomy of Educational Objectives; concerned with feelings, attitudes, and emotions rather than with cognitive processes or psychomotor skills

basal readers: a series of graded reading materials

behavioral objectives: the changes in a student's behavior that you hope will occur after a particular lesson

cloze test: a text with missing words that the student must fill in; a test of reading comprehension

cognitive processing: mental actions used to manipulate information in order to learn (the cognitive product) and then perform

criterion-referenced test: as opposed to norm-referenced test; grading based on specific, measurable standards

Brown v. Topeka Board of Education: 1954 Supreme Court case that ended the "separate but equal" doctrine and forced racial integration in public schools

divergent thinking: finds several different solutions to a problem rather than a single "right" solution

empirical research: based on observation, experience, or experiment

Education for All Handicapped Children Act of 1975 (EAHCA): mandated that all disabled children receive free, public, individualized and appropriate education in the least restrictive environment

First Amendment to the Constitution: guarantees the separation of church and state; the Supreme Court decision against school prayer was based on this amendment

flexible grouping: lesson planning that allows for students to work in large groups, small groups, or individually

formative evaluation: as opposed to summative evaluation, formative evaluation occurs during the process of developing a learning program

IEP: Individualized Education Program; developed in consultation with the parents of a disabled child who is to be moved into a regular classroom

kinesthetic learning: information gained and mastered through physical movement

least restrictive environment: mandated for all disabled children entering classrooms; prohibits unnecessary limits on physical movement or on participation in classroom activities

mainstreaming: placing a disabled student in a regular classroom

mastery learning theory: the idea that *all* students should be allowed time to thoroughly learn *all* the material being presented

mean, median, and mode: ways to evaluate student performance on graded tests; the *mean* is the common average of the numbers; the *median* is the number that is in the middle when the numbers are ordered; the *mode* is the number that appears most frequently in the group

norm-referenced test: grading based on how a student performs relative to other students in the class

Piaget: educational theorist who proposed that children learn through *organization* and *adaptation* in four developmental states: *sensorimotor*, *preoperational*, *concrete operations*, and *formal operations*

CRACKING THE QUESTIONS

First, thank your personal deity that you are taking a standardized test. Here's why: You can finesse your way to a lot of right answers that you wouldn't get if you had to come up with the answer on your own. That's because the key to getting the correct answer is right there in the question, if you know how to look for it.

How Do I Do That?

In three steps:

1. Read the question carefully. Make sure you know precisely what the question is asking for. Paraphrase it, but don't embroider it.

2. Look for the key phrase. Some word or phrase will narrow the scope of the question, giving you the specific topic involved. Make sure you identify it before looking at the answer choices.

3. Use POE.

It's that simple. Here's an example:

> An English teacher has given a test on an instructional unit introducing metaphor and simile. Which of the following test results would indicate that the material in the unit should be re-taught?
>
> (A) A third of the class was unable to quote lines of poetry containing various figures of speech.
>
> (B) Just under half of the class could not make up a short example of a metaphor or a simile.
>
> (C) More than half of the class was unable to write an essay comparing the use of metaphor in the poetry of different cultures.
>
> (D) When asked to write their own poems using either a metaphor or a simile, more than half of the class produced work that was stilted and unfinished.
>
> (E) Almost everyone in the class could not match lines of poetry to their authors.

Here's how to crack it

First, read the question really carefully. Paraphrase it: Which test result means the teacher blew it? And what was the teacher teaching? An introductory unit on metaphor and simile. That's the key phrase. Now look at the answers. (A) is about quoting lines—eliminate it. (B) looks pretty good—if almost half the class can't make up one measly example, they must not understand what a metaphor or a simile is. Not only is (C) about comparing poetry of different cultures, but it's an advanced task, not an introductory one—eliminate it. (D) is about the artistic talent or motivation of the students—eliminate it. (E) is about matching authors to quotes—eliminate it.

In other words, if you're teaching an intro to metaphor, your students should then know what a metaphor is. Nothing more, nothing less. The wrong answers may present things that would be good to know or interesting to know, but they don't answer the question. Focus very closely on what is asked and on the scope of the question. Eliminate everything that falls outside that scope.

QUICK QUIZ

What's the key phrase in each of the following questions?
The answers are on page 117.

The answers are on page 117.

1. A Spanish teacher whose instructional objective is that his students be able to respond appropriately in Spanish to a series of oral questions would be most successful if he implemented which of the following?

2. A teacher finds that generally the students in her biology class like some topics better than others and that among all the students, some topics appeal to some of them but not to others. If the teacher is planning to assign a term paper, which of the following would be the best way to do so?

3. Which of the following activities would require students to employ the lowest level of cognitive processing?

Not-So-Old Movies About Inspirational Teachers

Dead Poets' Society (you gotta love that Robin).
Dangerous Minds (you gotta love that Michelle).
Stand and Deliver (you gotta love that Edward).

CRACKING THE ANSWER CHOICES: SIX THINGS TO ELIMINATE RIGHT OFF THE BAT

Sometimes the test writers get tired and they run out of ideas for wrong answers. Some of these answers will be wrong every time, no matter what the question is. Immediately eliminate:

1. Any answer that advises a teacher to provoke a parent or administrator directly. Instead, look for answers that show tactful good manners and promote better communication.

2. Any answer that advises a teacher to hit a student, speak sarcastically to a student, or correct a student's every word. Sure, some teachers do those things, but that doesn't make it right—and they won't be right answers on the NTE either.

3. Any answer that puts standardized tests in a negative light. Hey, you're taking a standardized test, remember? The test writers aren't going to say that their own work is useless. (However, the test writers don't claim that standardized tests are appropriate for all testing purposes and situations.)

4. Any answer that advises a teacher to sit back and hope the problem goes away. Instead, look for answers that promote an active approach to problem solving.

5. Any answer that advises a teacher to favor one group of students over another. For instance, the gifted students should not be released from classroom chores that the other students are required to do. And the teacher should not gear her class to the slowest students and expect the others to take care of themselves.

6. Any answer that says a person with a lot of advanced degrees is better qualified than anyone else. People seem to be attracted to this kind of answer, possibly because it seems to have the authority of a Ph.D. But the NTE is not going to say that Ph.D.s should decide the fate of the world, or anything else for that matter.

Professional Knowledge Bonus Round #2

Who liked to call himself the Education President?

SUMMARY

1. Review the list of terms, or better yet, go through a couple of your best textbooks from class to refamiliarize yourself with material you may have studied a while back.

2. Don't worry if you have no idea how to answer a short fact-based question. If there aren't any key words in the question, take a quick guess and move on.

3. Read the question carefully and make sure you understand it exactly.

4. Before looking at the answer choices, look for key phrases in the question that indicate the precise topic (the scope) of the question.

5. Use POE. Eliminate any answer that falls outside the scope of the question. Remember that a single word is enough to make an entire answer wrong. Look for reasons to eliminate answers, rather than justifications for picking a particular answer.

6. Review the list of Six Things to Eliminate Right Off the Bat and make sure you do just that.

Answer

President George Herbert Walker Bush

CHAPTER 14—QUICK QUIZ ANSWERS

1. Respond in Spanish to oral questions.

2. Some topics appeal to some students but not to others.

3. Lowest level of cognitive processing.

PART **VI**

The Princeton Review
Diagnostic Test

Core Battery:
Test of
General Knowledge

This test book is divided into four separate sections. You will find a time limit printed at the beginning of each of the four sections. During the time indicated, you are to work on that section <u>only</u>. The supervisor will tell you when to begin and when to end each section. If you finish a section before time is called, you may check your work on that section, but you may <u>not</u> work on any of the other sections.

Work as rapidly as you can without sacrificing accuracy. Do not spend too much time puzzling over a question that seems too difficult for you. Answer the easier questions first; then return to the harder ones. <u>Try to answer every question even if you have to guess.</u> <u>Your score will be based on the number of questions you answer correctly. Unanswered questions will be counted in the same way as wrong answers.</u>

Where necessary, you may use blank spaces in the test book for scratch paper. Do not use any other paper or the margins or back of the answer sheet to do scratchwork.

YOU MUST INDICATE ALL OF YOUR ANSWERS ON THE SEPARATE ANSWER SHEET. No credit will be given for anything written in this test book. After you have decided which of the suggested answers is best, fill in the corresponding lettered space on the answer sheet. BE SURE THAT EACH MARK IS HEAVY AND DARK AND COMPLETELY FILLS THE ANSWER SPACE. Light or partial marks may not be read by the scoring machine.

EXAMPLE:

<u>Sample Answer</u>

Which of the following is the capital of the United States?

(A)   New York, NY
(B)   Washington, DC
(C)   Chicago, IL
(D)   Los Angeles, CA
(E)   Boston, MA

Give only one answer to each question. If you change an answer, be sure that the previous mark is erased <u>completely</u>. Incomplete erasures may be read as intended answers.

Time Limits

SECTION 1	30 minutes
SECTION 2	30 minutes
SECTION 3	30 minutes
SECTION 4	30 minutes
Total	120 minutes

SECTION 1

SOCIAL STUDIES

Time–30 minutes

Directions: Each of the questions or incomplete statements below is followed by five suggested answers or completions. Select the one that is best in each case and then fill in the corresponding lettered space on the answer sheet with a heavy, dark mark so that you cannot see the letter.

Remember, try to answer every question.

1. The right to vote is called

 (A) naturalization
 (B) suffrage
 (C) consolidation
 (D) democracy
 (E) disenfranchisement

2. Which of the following is an accurate description of the Monroe Doctrine?

 (A) It promoted open trade in China so that America and Europe would have access to important raw materials.
 (B) It asserted that Communism, once established, would spread to adjoining countries
 (C) It claimed the area surrounding the Panama Canal as an American territory
 (D) It tried to prevent European intervention and colonization in Latin America
 (E) It annexed the land now known as Texas from Mexico

3. Which of the following events is an example of collective bargaining?

 (A) The International Ladies' Garment Workers Union negotiated higher wages and improved working conditions from their employers
 (B) Despite higher interest rates for loans and evidence that consumer spending was plummeting, speculators continued to pour money into the stock market through the fall of 1929
 (C) In 1945, Franklin Roosevelt and Winston Churchill met with Joseph Stalin in Yalta to resolve issues of authority and control that threatened the coalition
 (D) The railway expansion of the late 19th century was funded, unlike the railways in Europe and Russia, almost entirely by private companies
 (E) In 1957, President Eisenhower forced the Governor of Arkansas, Orval Faubus, to withdraw the National Guard and allow black children to attend the previously segregated Central High School

GO ON TO THE NEXT PAGE.

Questions 4-5 are based on the following chart.

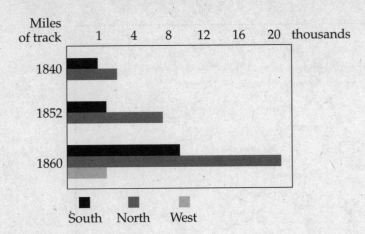

Miles of track — thousands: 1, 4, 8, 12, 16, 20

1840, 1852, 1860

■ South ■ North ■ West

4. It can be inferred from the chart that southern railroad development

   (A) would eventually equal that of the North
   (B) put the South at a distinct disadvantage during the Civil War
   (C) was adequate for the amount of cargo transport needed
   (D) increased faster during the 1840s than during the 1850s
   (E) began after railroads were developed in the West

5. According to the chart, which of the following statements is true about the period from 1850 to 1860?

   (A) The western railway system nearly doubled in size
   (B) The northern railway system surpassed that of the South
   (C) Although it had nearly doubled in the previous decade, the number of miles in the northern railway system increased only as much as the new western railroad
   (D) If the southern railway and the western railway were combined they would equal the length of the northern railway
   (E) Although it more than quadrupled, the number of miles of track in the South was still less than half that in the North

6. Which of the following would most likely be the work of a demographer?

   (A) An essay describing and analyzing the artwork of a small African settlement
   (B) A series of maps showing the evolution of national boundaries in Europe
   (C) A collection of data showing the population distribution of all the counties in a particular state
   (D) A speech advocating free college education for all American citizens
   (E) A quantitative analysis of current consumer prices

7. B. F. Skinner is known for

   (A) his work on operant conditioning, which led to the development of behavior modification techniques
   (B) being the first sociologist to apply psychological theory to his work
   (C) developing humanistic psychotherapy, in which the therapist takes an optimistic, integrated approach to the patient
   (D) the discovery of the unconscious
   (E) his theories of personality development, which have influenced the subsequent work of educators, sociologists, and psychologists

8. Explaining his concept of a Great Society, Lyndon Johnson said it "asks not only how much, but how good; not only how to create wealth, but how to use it; not only how fast we are going, but where we are headed. It proposes as the first test for a nation: the quality of its people."

   From the quotation above, it can be inferred that Johnson would have agreed with which of the following statements?

   (A) Social improvements can only occur after economic prosperity
   (B) Technological advances are a critical ingredient of national growth
   (C) An immoral nation will never enjoy long-term financial success
   (D) A society that develops slowly is more likely to be characterized by equality
   (E) Society can be improved through the efforts of its members

   GO ON TO THE NEXT PAGE.

Questions 9-10 are based on the following map.

9. According to the map, which of the following groups of countries had different borders in 1914 than in 1922?

(A) Portugal, Italy, Germany, and Greece
(B) France, Spain, Poland, and Rumania
(C) Italy, Rumania, and Poland
(D) Italy, Albania, and Turkey
(E) Bulgaria, Latvia, and Switzerland

10. The changes in borders and the formation of new nations came about as a result of

(A) World War I
(B) World War II
(C) the Franco-Prussian War
(D) the War of the Austrian Succession
(E) the War of the Roses

GO ON TO THE NEXT PAGE.

11. Which of the following is an example of a result of inflation?

(A) Congress votes not to raise the minimum wage for the next three years

(B) The price of bread drops because of an oversupply of wheat

(C) The number of new homes built does not rise for a period of eighteen months

(D) The average price of a new car increases by 40% in one year

(E) The average salary of an executive rises, while that of blue-collar workers stagnates

12. All of the following contributed to the strengthening of the movement for racial equality during the 1960s EXCEPT

(A) reaction to the murder of Medgar Evers

(B) Martin Luther King's speech during the Washington March

(C) the formation of groups such as CORE and SNCC

(D) the decline in the unemployment rate

(E) freedom riders

Questions 13-14 are based on the following chart.

13. Which of the following statements is true about the period from 1935 to 1957?

(A) The death rate increased slightly

(B) The birth rate and the death rate increased significantly

(C) The total population remained about the same

(D) The birth rate increased by more than half

(E) There were more deaths per thousand people than births per thousand people

14. All of the following could account for part of the changes documented in the chart EXCEPT

(A) an increase in immigration

(B) the discovery of penicillin

(C) the introduction of the polio vaccine

(D) better surgical techniques

(E) improved nutrition

GO ON TO THE NEXT PAGE.

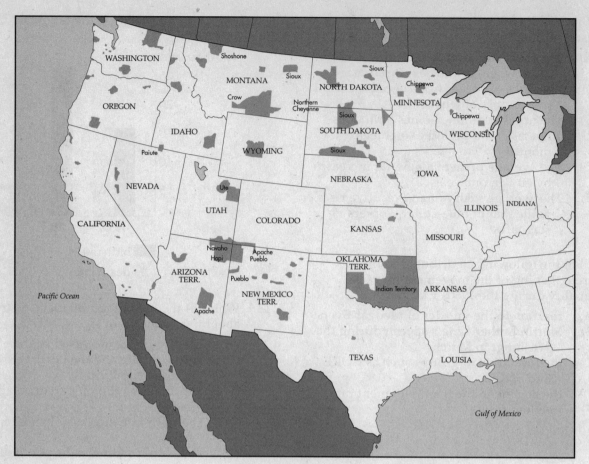

15. The creation of the reservations for Native American tribes shown in the map above can best be explained by which of the following statements?

(A) The United States government was making every effort to provide Native Americans with ample land to make up for their historical displacement

(B) Native Americans had always been concentrated in desert areas

(C) Native American tribes won more land during the period from 1875 to 1900 through both violent conflict and negotiation with the government

(D) Mining interests and the expansion of the population westward led the federal government to forcibly restrict Native Americans to lands chosen by the government

(E) Native American settlements in the East were minimal even before the United States was formed

GO ON TO THE NEXT PAGE.

16. "The right of citizens of the United States to vote in any primary or other election for President or Vice President, for electors for President or Vice President, or for Senator or Representative in Congress, shall not be denied or abridged by the United States or any State by reason of failure to pay any poll tax or other tax."

The above quotation is part of the 24th Amendment to the United States Constitution, adopted in 1964. Which of the following statements best applies to the Amendment?

(A) In response to pressure from voters, Congress had been trying numerous means to lower taxes
(B) Requiring citizens to pay money before voting had been used as a way to discourage poor people from exercising their right to vote, especially poor minorities
(C) The Amendment was strongly supported by Southern states
(D) Since the poll tax was not universally charged, Congress believed it should be abolished
(E) Although the Amendment forbids poll taxes for federal elections, it encourages poll taxes for local elections

Questions 17-18 refer to the following chart and the set of lettered statements below.

Year	Radio Stations	TV Stations
1950	2,773	70
1960	4,133	640
1970	6,760	2,490
1980	8,566	4,225
1990	10,819	9,575
1995	11,080	11,351

(A) The statement is probably true
(B) The statement is definitely true
(C) The statement is probably false
(D) The statement is definitely false
(E) There is insufficient information to evaluate the statement

Based on the information in the chart, choose the lettered statement that best describes each of the following.

17. Television stations first outpaced radio stations after 1955.

18. By 1970, television revenue was more than double that of radio because households spent more time watching television than listening to the radio

19. The Social Security Act was passed during the presidency of
(A) Theodore Roosevelt
(B) Woodrow Wilson
(C) Calvin Coolidge
(D) Herbert Hoover
(E) Franklin Roosevelt

GO ON TO THE NEXT PAGE.

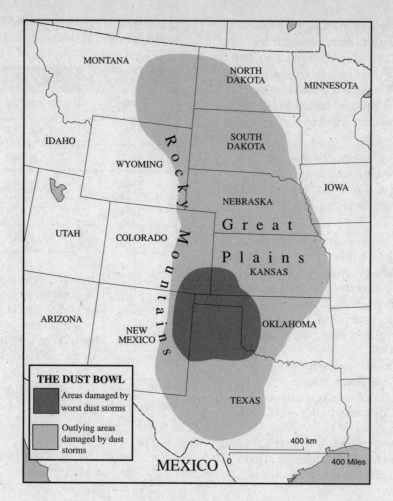

MONTANA

NORTH DAKOTA

MINNESOTA

IDAHO

SOUTH DAKOTA

WYOMING

IOWA

NEBRASKA

R o c k y   M o u n t a i n s

G r e a t

UTAH

COLORADO

P l a i n s

KANSAS

ARIZONA

NEW MEXICO

OKLAHOMA

THE DUST BOWL

Areas damaged by worst dust storms

Outlying areas damaged by dust storms

TEXAS

400 km

0   400 Miles

MEXICO

20. As part of the Hundred Days legislation, President Roosevelt and Congress provided for the creation of which of the following organizations that could address the problems depicted in the map?

(A) the Glass-Steagall Act
(B) the Civilian Conservation Corps
(C) the Tennessee Valley Authority
(D) the Farmer's Holiday Association
(E) the Public Works Administration

GO ON TO THE NEXT PAGE.

THE UNBLOODED POLITICAL PRIZE FIGHT.

21. The cartoon above is most likely dated

(A) 1820
(B) 1850
(C) 1860
(D) 1865
(E) 1910

22. Religious freedom in the United States is guaranteed by

(A) the 18th Amendment to the Constitution
(B) the Supreme Court decision in *Marbury v. Madison*
(C) the Bill of Rights
(D) the Declaration of Independence
(E) state laws

23. James Madison, Alexander Hamilton, and John Jay are known for their collaboration on

(A) the Federalist Papers
(B) the preamble to the Constitution
(C) the Articles of Confederation
(D) *The Rights of Man*
(E) the Declaration of Independence

GO ON TO THE NEXT PAGE.

Questions 24-25 are based on the following map.

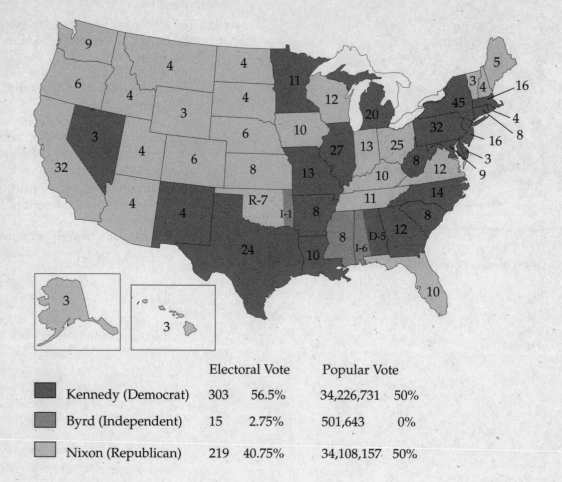

	Electoral Vote		Popular Vote	
Kennedy (Democrat)	303	56.5%	34,226,731	50%
Byrd (Independent)	15	2.75%	501,643	0%
Nixon (Republican)	219	40.75%	34,108,157	50%

24. Which of the following regions was LEAST consistent in its support for Presidential candidates in 1960?

(A) The Northwest
(B) The Midwest
(C) The South
(D) The Northeast
(E) The Southwest

25. According to the map, a citizen who voted for Nixon rather than Kennedy was more likely to

(A) live in the East
(B) be a registered Democrat
(C) have voted for Adlai Stevenson in 1952
(D) live in a state with a respectively smaller population
(E) live in a large city

GO ON TO THE NEXT PAGE.

26. A person who believed in social Darwinism would be LEAST likely to approve of which of the following?

(A) A small business is forced to close when its competitors steal its customers by offering lower prices.

(B) Valedictorian of her class, a woman earns a scholarship to a prestigious university.

(C) The federal government gives grant money to a struggling corporation.

(D) A corporation buys another corporation, fires thousands of its employees, and consequently earns record profits.

(E) A group of homeowners sues a chemical company for dumping toxic materials near the town's water supply.

Questions 27-28 are based on the following information.

For a number of reasons, the birth rate in the United States declined in the 1970s. One effect of this declining birth rate, as well as of the increase in life expectancy, was that the proportion of old people in the population became significantly larger.

27. If the total population of the United States steadily increased during the 1970s, which of the following could account for such an increase?

(A) Inflation
(B) Immigration
(C) A rise in the median annual salary
(D) A decrease in the death rate
(E) The availability of birth control

28. Which of the following is LEAST likely to have been a cause of the decline of the birth rate?

(A) The society as a whole was apprehensive about unstable economic and political conditions.
(B) A higher percentage of women entered the work force.
(C) Birth control became widely available.
(D) Population growth was concentrated in the South and West.
(E) Women were marrying at an older age.

Questions 29-30 are based on the following passage.

One of the ironies of modern life is that many more people live in cities than did in previous centuries, yet when the population density becomes quite high, people are more socially isolated than were their more rural forebears. In farming communities and small towns, people naturally are dependent on each other for help of various kinds, partly because they are more vulnerable to the vagaries of weather and nature itself, and partly because the communites are small enough that each individual has an identity known to everyone else. City-dwellers, on the other hand, often suffer from what can seem to be an anonymous existence; they may work in an enormous tower, along with thousands of other people unknown to them, and consequently their work and indeed their very lives may seem unimportant, indistinguishable from anyone else's.

29. According to the author, which of the following is an irony of modern life?

(A) Nature has more influence in the country than it does in the city.

(B) The more money a person makes, the more likely it is that he or she will feel unsatisfied.

(C) Although people who live in small towns know each other from an early age, there is no guarantee that they will like each other.

(D) The more crowded living conditions are, the more likely it is that the people living there will feel isolated from each other.

(E) When city-dwellers work in big office-buildings, they may develop low-level depression or anxiety.

30. The sociological effect described by the author has occurred LEAST in which of the following countries?

(A) Russia
(B) New Zealand
(C) Germany
(D) United States
(E) Great Britain

STOP

THIS IS THE END OF THE SOCIAL STUDIES SECTION.
IF YOU FINISH BEFORE TIME IS CALLED, YOU MAY CHECK YOUR WORK ON THIS SECTION ONLY.
DO NOT WORK ON ANY OTHER SECTION IN THE TEST.

NO TEST MATERIAL ON THIS PAGE.

SECTION 2

MATHEMATICS

Time–30 minutes

Directions: Each of the questions or incomplete statements below is followed by five suggested answers or completions. Select the one that is best in each case and then fill in the corresponding lettered space on the answer sheet with a heavy, dark mark so that you cannot see the letter.

Remember, try to answer every question.

1. At a hot dog stand, a bag of potato chips costs $0.75, sodas cost $1.00 each, and hot dogs cost $1.00 each. If Ralph wants to spend exactly $3.75, which of the following combinations can he buy?

(A)   1 hot dog, 2 bags of potato chips, and a soda
(B)   2 hot dogs and 2 sodas
(C)   2 hot dogs and 2 bags of potato chips
(D)   2 hot dogs, 1 bag of potato chips, and a soda
(E)   3 hot dogs, 1 bag of potato chips, and a soda

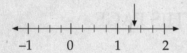

2. On the number line above, the arrow points closest to which of the following points?

(A) $-\dfrac{1}{2}$

(B)   1

(C) $1\dfrac{1}{4}$

(D) $1\dfrac{7}{8}$

(E)   2

3. Which of the following equations represents the statement "P is half of Q"?

(A) $Q = 2P$

(B) $\dfrac{P}{2} = Q$

(C) $QP = 2$

(D) $P - \dfrac{1}{2} = Q$

(E) $\dfrac{Q}{2} = 2P$

4. In the pattern above, each square has an area of 16. What is the combined area of the shaded regions?

(A)   16
(B)   24
(C)   36
(D)   40
(E)   54

5. Which of the following equations is correct?

(A) $.001 \times 1 = .01$
(B) $.01 \times 100 = 1$
(C) $.01 \times 10 = 1$
(D) $.001 \times 10 = .1$
(E) $.001 \times 100 = 10$

6. Chris wants to give each of his goats 25 square feet of pasture. What is the maximum number of goats that he can put in a rectangular pasture measuring 8 feet by 10 feet?

(A)   2

(B) $2\dfrac{1}{2}$

(C)   3

(D) $3\dfrac{1}{2}$

(E)   4

GO ON TO THE NEXT PAGE.

7. Marie wants to leave a 15% tip for her waiter at the end of her meal. If her bill is $7.00, which of the following operations will result in the correct tip?

(A) $.15 \times 7$

(B) 1.5×7

(C) $\dfrac{15}{10} \times 7$

(D) $\dfrac{7}{100} \div 7$

(E) $7 \div \dfrac{100}{15}$

Martha's Salary and Household Expenses

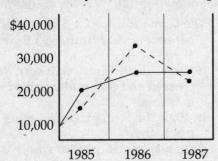

8. In the chart above, Martha's yearly salary is represented by a solid line and her expenses by a dotted line. By approximately how much money did Martha's expenses exceed her salary in 1986?

(A) $1,000
(B) $2,500
(C) $5,000
(D) $7,500
(E) $10,000

9. A teacher invented a game with the following rules:

1. Player 1 shouts out a number

2. Player 2 adds 2 to the number and claps if the new number is odd

3. Player 3 adds 1 to the new number, and stands up if the resulting number is divisible by 3

If Player 1 shouts out "Three!", which of the following will happen if all of the players follow the rules correctly?

(A) Player 2 does not clap, but Player 3 stands up
(B) Player 2 claps, but Player 3 does not stand up
(C) Player 2 stands up, and Player 3 claps
(D) Player 2 does not stand up, but Player 3 claps
(E) Player 2 claps, and Player 3 stands up

10. After Dolores is given a cake, she decides to share it with Anna. When Maribeth arrives, they each give her some of the cake. If Dolores has the most cake, and Anna the least, which of the following could be the respective fractional parts of the cake that Dolores, Maribeth, and Anna now have?

(A) $\dfrac{4}{9}, \dfrac{1}{3}, \dfrac{2}{9}$

(B) $\dfrac{1}{2}, \dfrac{1}{8}, \dfrac{3}{8}$

(C) $\dfrac{5}{6}, \dfrac{1}{6}, \dfrac{1}{6}$

(D) $\dfrac{3}{8}, \dfrac{1}{2}, \dfrac{1}{8}$

(E) $\dfrac{4}{9}, \dfrac{2}{9}, \dfrac{1}{3}$

GO ON TO THE NEXT PAGE.

11. Which of the following fractions is greatest?

(A) $\dfrac{5}{7}$

(B) $\dfrac{1}{2}$

(C) $\dfrac{11}{15}$

(D) $\dfrac{99}{100}$

(E) $\dfrac{3}{2}$

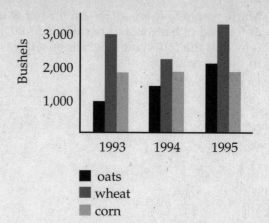

oats
wheat
corn

12. If the price of 6 potatoes is n, and the price of 3 turnips is a, what is the total cost of 3 potatoes and 6 turnips?

(A) $(n + a) \div \dfrac{3}{6}$

(B) $(n + a) \times 3$

(C) $3n + 6a$

(D) $2n + 6a$

(E) $\dfrac{n}{2} + 2a$

13. The chart above shows the grain production of Bluestone Farm from 1993 to 1995. Which of the following statements is correct?

(A) The farm produced the same amount of oats every year from 1993 through 1995

(B) In 1994, the production of corn decreased and the production of wheat increased

(C) In 1993, the farm produced more wheat than corn

(D) Corn was the only grain whose production decreased and then increased from 1993 to 1995

(E) The farm has always produced more oats than wheat

GO ON TO THE NEXT PAGE.

14. A math teacher gave a quiz with a total of 24 questions. If Joe answered every question, which of the following could NOT be the ratio of correct answers to incorrect answers on Jose's quiz?

    (A) 3 to 4
    (B) 5 to 1
    (C) 1 to 1
    (D) 3 to 1
    (E) 5 to 3

15. 2.01032 is between which of the following pairs of numbers?

    (A) 1.004 and 1.0673
    (B) 1.6032 and 2.00164
    (C) 2.0102 and 2.0107
    (D) 2.0111 and 2.0123
    (E) 2.0204 and 2.1036

16. If 2 and 9 are both factors of x, then x must be

    (A) odd
    (B) positive
    (C) a multiple of 18
    (D) a factor of 9 or 2
    (E) divisible by 11

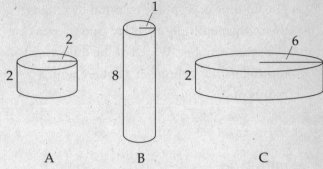

A   B   C

Note: Figures not drawn to scale.

17. The formula for the volume of a cylinder is $\pi r^2 h$, where r is the radius and h is the height. Based on the figures above, which of the following statements is true?

    I. The volume of A is equal to the volume of B
    II. The volume of B is less than the volume of A
    III. The volume of C is greater than the volumes of A and B

    (A) I only
    (B) II only
    (C) III only
    (D) I and III only
    (E) II and III only

18. A rope is to be cut into three lengths. The first is three times as long as the second, and the third is half as long as the first. If no rope is left over, which of the following could be the length, in feet, of the uncut rope?

    (A) 6
    (B) 7
    (C) 10
    (D) 11
    (E) 14

GO ON TO THE NEXT PAGE.

19. The volume of a sphere is found by cubing the radius, multiplying by π, and then taking $\frac{4}{3}$ of that number. Which of the following represents the volume of a sphere with a radius of 2?

(A) $\frac{4}{3}(2 \times 3)\pi$

(B) $\frac{4}{3}\left(\pi 2^3\right)$

(C) $2^3\left(\frac{3}{4}\pi\right)$

(D) $\left(\frac{2}{3} \times \frac{4}{3}\right)\pi$

(E) $\dfrac{\pi \frac{4}{3}}{3^2}$

20. A certain jogging trail is 5 miles long. If Marco and Sophie jog to the end of the trail, and Marco jogs twice as fast as Sophie, which of the following statements is true?

(A) Sophie will have jogged $2\frac{1}{2}$ miles before Marco reaches the end of the trail

(B) Marco jogs 5 miles per hour faster than Sophie

(C) Marco will reach the end of the trail in $\frac{2}{5}$ of an hour

(D) Marco will reach the end of the trail in half the time it will take Sophie

(E) Marco will reach the end of the trail in twice the time it will take Sophie

21. A certain machine produces 2 bolts per second. If the machine is operated continuously, approximately how long will it take to produce 175,000 bolts?

(A) 12 hours
(B) 1 day
(C) 1 week
(D) 1 month
(E) 1 year

22. Which of the following could NOT be folded to form a pyramid?

(A)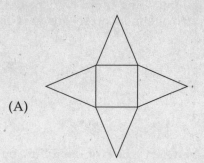

(B)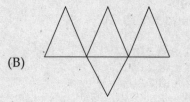

(C)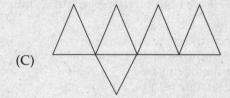

(D)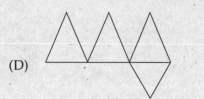

(E)

23. 10% of 300 is equal to 50% of

(A) 50
(B) 60
(C) 75
(D) 150
(E) 1500

GO ON TO THE NEXT PAGE.

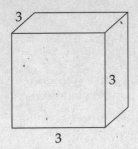

24. If the sides and top of the cardboard box shown above were cut so that the box was flattened into a single layer, the perimeter of the flat piece of cardboard would be

(A)   less than 9
(B)   between 9 and 24
(C)   between 25 and 30
(D)   between 31 and 40
(E)   greater than 40

25. A number that is divisible only by itself and 1 is called a prime number. Which of the following numbers CANNOT be prime?

(A) x
(B) $x + 1$
(C) $x + 2$
(D) $2x$
(E) $x - 2$

S T O P
THIS IS THE END OF THE MATHEMATICS SECTION.
IF YOU FINISH BEFORE TIME IS CALLED, YOU MAY CHECK YOUR WORK ON THIS SECTION ONLY.
DO NOT WORK ON ANY OTHER SECTION IN THE TEST.

SECTION 3
LITERATURE AND FINE ARTS
Time–30 minutes

Directions: Each of the questions or incomplete statements below is followed by five suggested answers or completions. Select the one that is best in each case and then fill in the corresponding lettered space on the answer sheet with a heavy, dark mark so that you cannot see the letter.

Remember, try to answer every question.

2. Which of the following gives the chateau pictured above the effect of solidity and heaviness?

 (A) The repetition of rectangular windows on the first and second floor
 (B) The steep, dark roof
 (C) The many chimneys of various heights
 (D) The contrast between large and small windows
 (E) The color of the stone with which it was built

1. The sculptor's rendering of all of the following help to give the impression that the figures in the sculpture above are in motion EXCEPT

 (A) their arms
 (B) their feet
 (C) his cloak
 (D) the leaves and branches at her feet
 (E) their hair

3. Which of the following is NOT a wind instrument?

 (A) Flute
 (B) Piccolo
 (C) Bassoon
 (D) Cello
 (E) Oboe

GO ON TO THE NEXT PAGE.

Questions 4-5 refer to the following.

There stands death, a bluish distillate
in a cup without a saucer. Such a strange
place to find a cup: standing on the back of a hand.
One recognizes clearly the line along the glazed
curve, where the handle snapped. Covered with
dust. And *HOPE* is written across the side, in faded
Gothic letters.

4. Which of the following is most emphasized
    by the poet's choice of metaphor?

    (A) The death was unexpected
    (B) The fact that death exists does not mean
         there is no hope
    (C) The poet is not afraid of his own death
    (D) Death is concrete and even mundane
    (E) The person who died was a stranger to
         the poet

5. The poet employs the image in the last
    sentence most probably in order to

    (A) assert that death does not affect him
    (B) produce an ironic effect
    (C) show that the cup was old
    (D) end the poem on an optimistic note
    (E) make the situation seem more realistic

Questions 6-8 refer to the following.

My father had a friend, old Baron von Bracken,
who had in his day traveled much and known
many cities and men. Otherwise, he was not at all
like Odysseus, and could least of all be called
ingenious, for he had shown very little skill in
managing his own affairs. Probably from a sense of
failure in this respect he carefully kept from discussing practical matters with an efficient younger
generation, keen on their careers and with success
in life. But on theology, the opera, moral right and
wrong, and other unprofitable pursuits he was a
pleasant talker.

6. The author makes an analogy to which of the
    following?

    (A) A god from Roman mythology
    (B) A contemporary writer
    (C) A character from *The Canterbury Tales*
    (D) The protagonist of a Shakespearean
         tragedy
    (E) The protagonist of a Greek epic

7. Which of the following statements about the
    narrator is indicated by the passage?

    (A) He vehemently dislikes the Baron
    (B) He attempts to understand what moti-
         vates the behavior of people he knows
    (C) He believes that succeeding in one's
         career is more important than main-
         taining social relationships
    (D) He does not generally approve of his
         father's friends
    (E) He fails to make a distinction between
         activities related to business and those
         related to frivolity

8. The narrator characterizes the Baron as
    someone who is

    (A) arrogant and spiteful
    (B) ancient and tedious
    (C) sophisticated and proud
    (D) philosophical and dull
    (E) crafty and mysterious

GO ON TO THE NEXT PAGE.

9. All of the following can be discerned in the painting above EXCEPT

(A) stylized brushwork that produces a cluttered effect

(B) the emotional state of the people depicted

(C) focus on the subjects' faces

(D) the influence of photography

(E) artists had begun to choose working class subjects

GO ON TO THE NEXT PAGE.

10. The painting above is characterized by

    (A) man's effort to control nature
    (B) a geometric composition that produces
         a lighthearted effect
    (C) an abstract treatment of both the sub-
         jects and the landscape
    (D) a depiction of the artist's morality
    (E) a reliance on classical themes

GO ON TO THE NEXT PAGE.

Questions 11-13 refer to the passages below.

(A)　You do not do, you do not do
　　　Any more, black shoe
　　　In which I have lived like a foot
　　　For thirty years, poor and white,
　　　Barely daring to breathe or Achoo.

(B)　Sports and gallantries, the stage, the
　　　arts, the antics of dancers,
　　　The exuberant voices of music,
　　　Have charm for children but lack
　　　nobility; it is bitter earnestness
　　　That makes beauty; the mind
　　　Knows, grown adult.

(C)　I've known rivers:
　　　I've known rivers ancient as the world
　　　and older than the
　　　　　flow of human blood in human veins.
　　　My soul has grown deep like the rivers.

(D)　I placed a jar in Tennessee,
　　　And round it was, upon a hill.
　　　It made the slovenly wilderness
　　　Surround that hill.

(E)　In Xanadu did Kubla Khan
　　　A stately pleasure dome decree:
　　　Where Alph, the sacred river, ran
　　　Through caverns measureless to man
　　　　　Down to a sunless sea.

11.　Which has a rhyme scheme?

12.　Which compares the poet to a part of the body?

13.　Which uses repetition to achieve a rhythmic effect?

14.　Which of the following is true of the phrases of music shown above?

　　(A)　The phrases are in different keys
　　(B)　The phrases are roughly symmetrical
　　(C)　The second is an exact retrograde of the first
　　(D)　The phrases have different timbres
　　(E)　There are fewer beats per measure in the first

GO ON TO THE NEXT PAGE.

Questions 15-16 refer to the following.

      She remained awake the rest of the night,
giving Port his pills regularly, and trying to
relax in the periods between. Each time she
woke him he moved obediently and swal-
(5) lowed the water and the tablet proffered him
without speaking or even opening his eyes. In
the pale, infected light of daybreak she heard
him begin to sob. Electrified, she sat up and
stared at the corner where his head lay. Her
(10) heart was beating very fast, activated by a
strange emotion she could not identify. She
listened awhile, decided it was compassion
she felt, and leaned nearer to him.

15.   Which of the following is the most accurate
description of the passage above?

(A)   A nurse in a small-town hospital takes
care of one of her patients

(B)   A man on his death-bed is forced to
depend on a woman he once wronged

(C)   A woman experiences confused emotions while helping a sick friend

(D)   While traveling, a husband and wife are
both infected with the same disease

(E)   As she nurses a friend back to health, a
woman recalls their shared past

16.   The phrase "the pale, infected light of
daybreak" (line 7) serves to

(A)   divert the reader's attention from the
seriousness of the situation by intro-
ducing a lyrical note

(B)   inform the reader that the characters
were living during a widespread
outbreak of a dangerous infectious
disease

(C)   indicate that the scene took place in
winter

(D)   suggest that the woman would soon be
affected by the same disease Port was
suffering from

(E)   show that Port's illness was affecting
the way the woman experienced the
rest of the world

GO ON TO THE NEXT PAGE.

<u>Questions 17-19</u> refer to the following.

(A)

(C)

(B)

(D)

GO ON TO THE NEXT PAGE.

(E)

17. Which of the buildings is oldest?

18. Practical utility was most important to the architect of which building?

19. Which of the following statements is the most accurate?
    (A) All of the buildings were designed for the same purpose
    (B) All of the exteriors are ornately decorated
    (C) All of the buildings have regularly spaced windows
    (D) At least one of the buildings was intended to be a place of worship
    (E) At least three of the buildings have domes

GO ON TO THE NEXT PAGE.

<u>Question 20</u> refers to the poem below.

Sweet rose, fair flower, untimely plucked, soon vaded,
Plucked in the bud, and vaded in the spring!
Bright orient pearl, alack, too timely shaded!
Fair creature, killed too soon by death's sharp sting!
　　Like a green plum that hangs upon a tree,
　　And falls through wind before the fall should be.

20. The poet's central theme is

　　(A)　the fading of beauty in old age
　　(B)　the cruelty of nature
　　(C)　the inevitability of death
　　(D)　the sorrow caused by an early death
　　(E)　the natural cycle of life and death

21. The architect of the house pictured above most probably designed the layered concrete balconies so that

　　(A)　the sun would enter the house from every window at some time during the day
　　(B)　the house would look like an impregnable fortress
　　(C)　their circular form would contrast with the rest of the house
　　(D)　trees and underbrush would eventually hide them from view
　　(E)　the house would seem to blend into the site by mimicking the natural outcroppings of rock

22. The dancer in the photograph above has contracted different parts of her body in order to produce

　　(A)　a sense of grandeur
　　(B)　sharp movements
　　(C)　a sense of slowed time
　　(D)　a typically romantic pose
　　(E)　a lyrical effect

GO ON TO THE NEXT PAGE.

Questions 24-26 refer to the following.

Turning and turning in the widening gyre
The falcon cannot hear the falconer;
Things fall apart; the center cannot hold;
Mere anarchy is loosed upon the world,
The blood-dimmed tide is loosed, and everywhere
The ceremony of innocence is drowned;
The best lack all conviction, while the worst
Are full of passionate intensity.

24. The poet's mood can best be described as

    (A) excited and happy
    (B) melancholy and lethargic
    (C) apprehensive and pessimistic
    (D) cold and unfeeling
    (E) cynical and distracted

23. Which of the following is the best characterization of the painting above?

    (A) The artist is most interested in narrative painting
    (B) The artist has a grim view of humanity
    (C) The hats worn by the subjects serve a symbolic function
    (D) The composition is intentionally out of balance
    (E) The overall effect is humorous

25. Which of the following does the poet employ in the first three lines?

    (A) Blank verse
    (B) Onomatopoeia
    (C) Assonance
    (D) Dramatic irony
    (E) End rhyme

26. The theme of the poem can best be described as

    (A) an expression of the poet's view of the state of the world
    (B) narrative, since it describes a particular historical event
    (C) self-referential
    (D) less important than its striking imagery
    (E) relatively small in scope

GO ON TO THE NEXT PAGE.

27. Which of the following statements best characterizes the photograph above?

(A) The man is uncomfortable with public speaking

(B) The photographer was attempting to capture a soft, flowing image

(C) The composition relies on linear and curved elements

(D) The viewer's eye is most drawn to the letters at the top left corner

(E) The immense poster image of the speaker has the effect of diminishing him

GO ON TO THE NEXT PAGE.

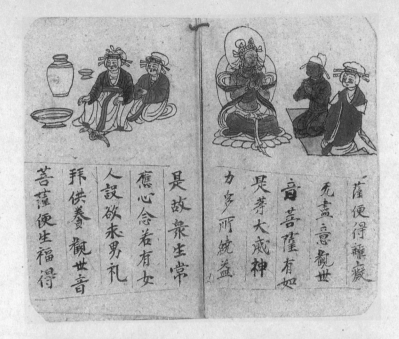

28. Which of the following is NOT a difference between the two Chinese paintings above?

(A) The subject matter
(B) The composition
(C) The width of brushstroke
(D) The attitude of the artist towards his subject
(E) The juxtaposition of writing with artwork

GO ON TO THE NEXT PAGE.

29. The cartoon was drawn in order to

   (A) comment on the benefits of the industrial revolution
   (B) mimic the style of Botticelli
   (C) demonstrate socialist sympathies toward the working class
   (D) convince the general public that there should be only one political party
   (E) demonstrate laziness among laborers in nineteenth century Europe

GO ON TO THE NEXT PAGE.

Questions 30-32 are based on the following passages.

(A)   He handed her the letter whose secrets he wanted to carry with him to the grave, but she put the folded sheets in her dressing table without reading them and locked the drawer with a key. She was accustomed to her husband's unfathomable capacity for astonishment, his exaggerated opinions that became more incomprehensible as the years went by, his narrowness of mind that was out of tune with his public image. But this time he had outdone himself.

(B)   Mrs. Penniman was a tall, thin, fair, rather faded woman, with a perfectly amiable disposition, a high standard of gentility, a taste for light literature, and a certain foolish indirectness and obliquity of character. She was romantic; she was sentimental; she had a passion for little secrets and mysteries—a very innocent passion, for her secrets had hitherto always been as impractical as addled eggs.

(C)   New Orleans is very beautiful and very painful. New York is not that beautiful and not that painful. It is just a normal American town. Whereas New Orleans has a caliber of beauty among the massive oaks, at times a vision of paradise, but there is an unvarnished truth about it, and there are your memories and those held dear.

(D)   Had there been an axe handy, or a poker, any weapon that would have gashed a hole in his father's breast and killed him, there and then, James would have seized it. Such were the extremes of emotion that Mr. Ramsay excited in his children's breasts by his mere presence; standing, as now, lean as a knife, narrow as the blade of one, grinning sarcastically, not only with the pleasure of disillusioning his son and casting ridicule upon his wife, who was ten thousand times better in every way than he was (James thought), but also with some secret conceit at his own accuracy of judgement.

(E)   The dog was everything a dog should not be. It looked too old to be alive, emaciated, flabby at the same time, and its stringy coat was patched with dried-on mud. I did not understand how Nicholas could get as close as he was to anything that looked the way the creature did. I had seen my brother shield his face in Mexican markets to block out slightly overripe papayas. Ordinarily, he was revolted by men in short-sleeved shirts; he had a horror of clip-on bow ties. Yet there he was, kneeling down beside the creature on the stone.

30.   Which makes use of vivid examples to describe a character trait?

31.   Which describes the effect a man has upon his family?

32.   In which of the following is the narrator surprised at someone else's behavior?

    (A)   A and B
    (B)   A and D
    (C)   A and E
    (D)   B and D
    (E)   D and E

GO ON TO THE NEXT PAGE.

Questions 33-35 refer to the following.

(A)

(C)

(B)

(D)

GO ON TO THE NEXT PAGE.

(E)

33. In which of the paintings is space created by overlapping layers rather than by foreshortening?

34. Which of the following elements do the paintings have in common?

(A) An obsessive attention to small details
(B) The elevation of linear over curved forms
(C) A pessimistic attitude towards society
(D) A highly subjective rendering of reality
(E) The superimposition of various shapes

35. During which of the following periods were all five paintings created?

(A) 1800-1850
(B) 1851-1900
(C) 1901-1940
(D) 1941-1960
(E) 1961-1990

S T O P

THIS IS THE END OF THE LITERATURE AND FINE ARTS SECTION.
IF YOU FINISH BEFORE TIME IS CALLED, YOU MAY CHECK YOUR WORK ON THIS SECTION ONLY.
DO NOT WORK ON ANY OTHER SECTION IN THE TEST.

SECTION 4
SCIENCE
Time–30 minutes

<u>Directions</u>: Each of the questions or incomplete statements below is followed by five suggested answers or completions. Select the one that is best in each case and then fill in the corresponding lettered space on the answer sheet with a heavy, dark mark so that you cannot see the letter.

Remember, try to answer every question.

1. Erosion results in all of the following EXCEPT

   (A) the loss of topsoil from farmlands
   (B) the gradual wearing down of mountain ranges
   (C) the depletion of groundwater reserves
   (D) the buildup of silt in the mouths of rivers
   (E) the weathering of rocks

2. Cell membranes are known to be selectively permeable. Which of the following is an example of this quality?

   (A) Red blood cells allow potassium ions to pass into them, but block out sodium ions, even though potassium and sodium ions are similar in size
   (B) The DNA embedded in a cell ensures that when the cell reproduces, it will form cells similar to itself
   (C) When a white blood cell surrounds bacteria, it digests the bacteria through the release of enzymes contained in the lysosomes
   (D) Since most than 90 percent of a cell is made of water, all cells have a fluid quality
   (E) Microtubules direct the flow of materials within the cytoplasm, creating passageways through which organelles may move

3. A battery runs by which of the following means?

   (A) Conservation of energy
   (B) Electrical storage of potential energy
   (C) Conversion of internal energy to kinetic energy
   (D) Conversion of mechanical energy to electrical energy
   (E) Conversion of chemical energy to electrical energy

4. The amount of cholesterol in a person's bloodstream may be affected by all of the following EXCEPT

   (A) consumption of aspirin
   (B) heredity
   (C) exercise
   (D) diet
   (E) smoking

5. White light is made up of every wavelength in the visible spectrum. When a beam of white light is passed through a prism, a rainbow results because

   (A) of structural flaws in the prism's glass
   (B) the wavelengths are fused within the prism
   (C) the colors in the beam do not bend equally
   (D) red rays and blue rays repel each other
   (E) a wavelength can change under certain conditions

6. The bone structure of which of the following is NOT similar to the others?

   (A) The paw of a bear
   (B) The flipper of a dolphin
   (C) The hand of a human being
   (D) The hoof of a horse
   (E) The wing of a bird

GO ON TO THE NEXT PAGE.

7. The medical community generally agrees that in order to keep fit and have a strong heart a person must
   (A) engage in some activity that raises the heart rate for at least 15 minutes, three times a week
   (B) engage in both aerobic and anaerobic activities every day
   (C) eat at least one helping of leafy greens each day
   (D) take both vitamin supplements and aspirin each day
   (E) jog or ride a stationary bicycle for 30 minutes, four times a week

8. Geologic evidence supports the theory that most of the land on Earth was originally part of one great land mass. The gradual splitting apart into separate land masses is caused by
   (A) extreme volcanic activity
   (B) disruptions of magnetic fields
   (C) continental drift
   (D) erosion
   (E) climatic changes

9. Which of the following statements about nutrition is correct?
   (A) Ingesting any type of fat contributes to high cholesterol
   (B) The major cause of hyperactivity in children is sugar
   (C) A vegetarian diet is almost always too low in protein
   (D) Vitamin C must be replaced every day because it is excreted, not stored
   (E) A diet high in beta carotene prevents and cures cancer

Questions 10-11 are based on the following.

An experiment tested the effects of using organic compost as fertilizer. The plants of each type were raised identically from the same seed source. The first group of plants received no application of fertilizer, while the second group received an application of compost when the plants were eight weeks old.

Average Number of Fruits or Vegetables Per Plant

	Control group	Compost group
Tomatoes	9.4	14.8
Eggplants	2.1	2.3
Peppers	2.3	4.1
Corn	.9	1.8
Potatoes	8.0	12.4

10. Based on the data recorded above, which of the following statements is true?
    (A) Compost is the best fertilizer available
    (B) Commercial chemical fertilizers may produce high yields, but they deplete rather than enrich the soil
    (C) Compost is a useful fertilizer for all fruit and vegetable plants
    (D) Although compost is an effective fertilizer for peppers, it is not as effective for tomatoes
    (E) For most of the plants in the experiment, compost was effective in raising yields

GO ON TO THE NEXT PAGE.

11. Which of the following, if overlooked by the conductor of the experiment, would have led to flawed data?

    (A) Temperatures dropped below 40 degrees after some of the tomatoes had flowered, which caused the flowers to drop

    (B) Because most of the tomatoes in the control group were planted close to a fence, they did not receive as much rain as the other tomatoes

    (C) Eggplants typically do not produce fruit if the average temperatures are not hot enough

    (D) Since corn uses a lot of nutrients to grow, it should be planted in fertile soil

    (E) Some peppers in both groups were killed by cutworms before the plants were eight weeks old

12. When two organisms with different traits are crossed, the trait that is found in their offspring is called the dominant trait. A blue-eyed, brown-haired, tall woman and a blue-eyed, blond, tall man have a daughter of average height, who has blue eyes, brown hair, and fair skin. Which of the following is the dominant trait in the daughter?

    (A) Her blue eyes
    (B) Her brown hair
    (C) Her gender
    (D) Her height
    (E) Her complexion

13. A magazine article states:

    "A total of 100,000 or more plants and animals are currently threatened with extinction, but many governments are unwilling to do what is necessary to preserve these valuable natural resources."

    A conservationist would most likely defend which of the following as the most effective means of doing "what is necessary" ?

    (A) Raising public awareness of the problem, which would reduce the market for illegal trade in endangered species

    (B) Providing zoos with enough resources that they can breed endangered species in captivity

    (C) Protecting large areas of land from development so that the complex ecosystems that sustain endangered species are preserved

    (D) Concentrating efforts to maintain healthy populations of the plants and animals that aren't endangered

    (E) Setting up government agencies to study each individual endangered species

14. Butterflies found in high mountain ranges are darker than those of related species found at lower altitudes. All of the following could be evolutionary explanations for the dark color EXCEPT

    (A) It protects the butterflies from predators
    (B) It protects the butterflies from the ultraviolet rays of the sun
    (C) It allows the butterflies to gather the maximum amount of heat from the sun
    (D) It allows the butterflies to withstand strong winds
    (E) It allows the butterflies to blend in with rocky surfaces

GO ON TO THE NEXT PAGE.

15. When a massive star collapses, it contracts and becomes denser until not even light can escape its gravitational field. Such an extreme collapse results in

   (A) a red giant
   (B) a black hole
   (C) a white dwarf
   (D) the formation of a planet
   (E) a neutron star

16. In studying the four-year population cycle of lemmings, a scientist would be interested in all of the following EXCEPT

   (A) the stability of their food supply
   (B) the size of the predator population
   (C) the ability of the species to dig burrows in winter that protect them from freezing
   (D) whether the lemmings have continuous access to water
   (E) whether climatic conditions in any one year were unfavorable to lemmings

17. After a roller coaster has descended a hill, it cannot then climb a hill equally high because

   (A) some of its potential energy has been lost through friction
   (B) gravity reduces its energy on the descent
   (C) gravitational forces are reduced on a smaller hill
   (D) the weight of the passengers reduces its potential energy
   (E) kinetic energy is always weaker than mechanical energy

18. If fossils show that an earlier relative of a species had long fangs, but the contemporary species has medium or short fangs, which of the following statements is most likely true?

   (A) The long fangs of the earlier species served no vital purpose
   (B) As the species continues to evolve, the fangs will become shorter and shorter
   (C) The encroachment of man on nearly every habitat has indirectly led to unnecessary adaptations in many animals
   (D) Long fangs are usually unwieldy, and used more to attract mates than to hunt successfully
   (E) The species no longer needs long fangs in order to survive

19. Which of the following is (are) necessary in the formation of a cloud?

   I.   Moist air rises and cools
   II. Convection currents are present a few hundred feet from the ground
   III. Microscopic dust particles are present in the atmosphere

   (A) I only
   (B) II only
   (C) III only
   (D) I and III only
   (E) I, II, and III

20. The moon revolves around the Earth once every 27.3 days, which is the same amount of time it takes to complete one rotation around its axis. Which of the following phenomena is a result of the fact that one revolution and one rotation of the moon each take 27.3 days to complete?

   (A) Oceanic tides are influenced by the moon
   (B) The moon is full only once a month
   (C) The same hemisphere of the moon always faces the Earth
   (D) When the moon passes into the Earth's shadow, it causes a lunar eclipse
   (E) The moon waxes and wanes over the course of each month

GO ON TO THE NEXT PAGE.

21. Responses of the skin to either hot or cold stimuli include which of the following?

    I. Dilation of blood vessels
    II. Evaporation of sweat
    III. Constriction of blood vessels

    (A) I only
    (B) II only
    (C) I and II only
    (D) II and III only
    (E) I, II, and III

22. Which represents the organism lowest on a food chain that includes all of the following?

    (A) Human beings
    (B) Fish
    (C) Shrimp
    (D) Algae
    (E) Bears

23. In Galileo's famous experiment, a cannon ball and a pebble hit the ground at the same time after being dropped simultaneously from the same height. Which of the following did the experiment prove?

    (A) Some objects resist downward movement because of increased air resistance
    (B) Objects of different masses have different rates of acceleration
    (C) Gravity causes the same rate of acceleration for all objects
    (D) If air resistance and gravitational force are equal, the velocity of the falling object is limited
    (E) Some energy in the downward fall is lost through friction with the air

24. Although water freezes at 32 degrees, sea water freezes at 28 degrees. What is the cause of the difference?

    (A) The salinity of sea water
    (B) The reduced intensity of sunlight as the sea deepens
    (C) The presence of sound waves in sea water
    (D) The effect of tides on the oceans
    (E) The relatively constant temperatures at the bottom of the ocean

25. Since its main source is seawater or kelp, a certain element necessary for metabolism control is added to a common seasoning. The element is

    (A) Vitamin A
    (B) Flourine
    (C) Iodine
    (D) Potassium
    (E) Selenium

26. Which of the following is the correct order of classification, from the largest group to the smallest?

    (A) Phylum, class, kingdom, order, family, genus, species
    (B) Kingdom, phylum, class, order, family, genus, species
    (C) Kingdom, class, order, genus, phylum, family, species
    (D) Kingdom, genus, class, order, phylum, species, family
    (E) Genus, kingdom, class, phylum, order, species, family

27. Which of the following is (are) characteristic of all living things?

    I. They are made up of cells
    II. They reproduce sexually
    III. They can move and grow

    (A) II only
    (B) I and II only
    (C) I and III only
    (D) II and III only
    (E) I, II, and III

GO ON TO THE NEXT PAGE.

28. The biological process by which larger molecules are built from smaller ones is called

    (A) osmosis
    (B) reproduction
    (C) mitosis
    (D) synthesis
    (E) fusion

29. Which of the following, if it happened, would have the greatest beneficial effect on air quality?

    (A) Laws are passed lowering the acceptable emission levels of certain dangerous gases from factories
    (B) The majority of people in the country drive electric rather than gas-powered cars
    (C) The majority of homeowners use oil rather than natural gas to heat their homes
    (D) The use of air conditioners is rationed so that on very hot days there is less chance that circuits will become overloaded
    (E) The number of smokers drops to only 5% of the population

30. All of the following statements about atoms are correct EXCEPT:

    (A) The atomic weight of an atom is the total mass of all its particles
    (B) Different isotopes of the same element have varying numbers of neutrons but the same number of protons
    (C) Isotopes of the same element have similar atomic weights and different chemical properties
    (D) Protons have a positive electrical charge
    (E) Atoms are composed of protons, electrons, and neutrons, but not every atom contains all three particles

S T O P

THIS IS THE END OF THE SCIENCE SECTION.
IF YOU FINISH BEFORE TIME IS CALLED, YOU MAY CHECK YOUR WORK ON THIS SECTION ONLY.
DO NOT WORK ON ANY OTHER SECTION IN THE TEST.

NO TEST MATERIAL ON THIS PAGE.

Core Battery:
Test of
Communication Skills

This test book is divided into four separate sections. You will find a time limit printed at the beginning of each of the four sections. During the time indicated, you are to work on that section <u>only</u>. The supervisor will tell you when to begin and when to end each section. If you finish a section before time is called, you may check your work on that section, but you may <u>not</u> work on any of the other sections.

Work as rapidly as you can without sacrificing accuracy. Do not spend too much time puzzling over a question that seems too difficult for you. Answer the easier questions first; then return to the harder ones. <u>Try to answer every question even if you have to guess. Your score will be based on the number of questions you answer correctly. Unanswered questions will be counted in the same way as wrong answers.</u>

Where necessary, you may use blank spaces in the test book for scratch paper. Do not use any other paper or the margins or back of the answer sheet to do scratchwork.

YOU MUST INDICATE ALL OF YOUR ANSWERS ON THE SEPARATE ANSWER SHEET. No credit will be given for anything written in this test book. After you have decided which of the suggested answers is best, fill in the corresponding lettered space on the answer sheet. BE SURE THAT EACH MARK IS HEAVY AND DARK AND COMPLETELY FILLS THE ANSWER SPACE. Light or partial marks may not be read by the scoring machine.

EXAMPLE:

<u>Sample Answer</u>

ⒶⒷ●ⒸⒹⒺ

Which of the following is the capital of the United States?

(A) New York, NY
(B) Washington, DC
(C) Chicago, IL
(D) Los Angeles, CA
(E) Boston, MA

Give only one answer to each question. If you change an answer, be sure that the previous mark is erased <u>completely</u>. Incomplete erasures may be read as intended answers.

Time Limits

SECTION 1	30 minutes
SECTION 2	30 minutes
SECTION 3	30 minutes
SECTION 4	30 minutes
Total	120 minutes

GO ON TO THE NEXT PAGE.

SECTION 1

LISTENING

Approximate time–30 minutes

Part A

<u>Directions</u>: There are two kinds of problems in Part A. One kind requires you to answer a short question, the other to show that you understand a short statement. <u>These questions and statements will be spoken just one time.</u> They are not written out in the test book, so you will have to listen carefully.

When you hear a <u>question</u>, read the four answers given in your test book and select the one you believe to be correct. Then, on your answer sheet, find the number of the problem and fill in the space containing the letter of the answer you have chosen. When you hear a <u>statement</u>, read the four sentences and decide which one is closest in meaning to or best supported by the statement. Then, on your answer sheet, find the number of the problem and mark your answer.

EXAMPLE:

You will hear: "How often do you go to the movies?"   <u>Sample Answer</u>

You will read: (A)   The theater's close. We usually walk.   Ⓐ Ⓑ ● Ⓓ
                   (B)   No. We don't go all that much.
                   (C)   Once every week or two.
                   (D)   Because we both enjoy movies.

Sentence (C), "Once every week or two," is the response to the question, "How often do you go to the movies?" Therefore, you should choose answer (C).

EXAMPLE:

You will hear: "James relaxed with a sigh of relief   <u>Sample Answer</u>
                   when he heard the news."   Ⓐ ● Ⓒ Ⓓ

You will read: (A)   The news was very disappointing
                   (B)   The news was better than expected
                   (C)   The news made James very sad
                   (D)   The news made James extremely nervous

Sentence (B), "The news was better than expected," is best supported by the statement, "James relaxed with a sigh of relief when he heard the news." Therefore, you should choose answer (B).

Now let us begin Part A. Try to respond to every problem. Be sure to mark all answers on your answer sheet and completely fill the lettered space with a heavy, dark mark so that you cannot see the letter.

1. (A)   Lucinda has never made a raspberry
              strudel
    (B)   Lucinda was confident that she knew
              how to make the strudel
    (C)   Lucinda thought that the recipe for the
              strudel was too complicated to follow
    (D)   The recipe for the strudel was in a
              cookbook for professional chefs

2. (A)   Jimmy had never done well in school
    (B)   Jimmy's report card was better than his
              parents expected it be
    (C)   Most of the time Jimmy brought home
              an impressive report card
    (D)   Jimmy's parents had not been con-
              cerned about how he was doing in
              school

GO ON TO THE NEXT PAGE.

3. (A) Last year I learned to play the piano by ear
   (B) I've always thought everyone should learn to play a musical instrument
   (C) It takes a lot of practice, but I'm making progress
   (D) I like banjo music much more than violin music

4. (A) Many students eventually embark on careers that require a knowledge of higher mathematics
   (B) For students to benefit from studying mathematics, they must have excellent teachers
   (C) Students can learn to think more logically by studying higher mathematics
   (D) Nothing a student learns in higher mathematics has any practical benefit

5. (A) Probably, since he will make more money in his new job
   (B) No, he was looking forward to the move
   (C) Some states have colder weather than Vermont does
   (D) I think he likes snow more than warmth, since skiing is his favorite hobby

6. (A) The concert does not begin for more than an hour
   (B) If we're late to the concert, we won't be allowed to take our seats
   (C) The concert begins in an hour and a half
   (D) We were late to the concert last month

7. (A) In addition to doing the workbook exercises, you must regularly listen to tapes in order to improve your listening skills
   (B) Some members of the class study French two days per week
   (C) It's a good idea to join the French club so that you can practice speaking French outside of class
   (D) You should spend some time each day studying French, even if it's only half an hour

8. (A) The students like some topics in physics class better than others
   (B) Some of the students studied harder for last week's test than for any of the previous tests
   (C) All of the students usually do well in physics
   (D) All of the students had gotten higher grades on previous physics tests

9. (A) The faculty meeting was postponed because so many teachers had the flu
   (B) The scheduling of faculty meetings is the responsibility of the principal
   (C) I didn't know the correct time of the faculty meeting
   (D) Faculty meetings are usually on Tuesday afternoons

10. (A) The committee needs to raise a lot more money than it did last year
    (B) Mary is a reliable worker
    (C) It was difficult to convince anyone to be on the fundraising committee
    (D) Mary has had experience in fundraising

11. (A) Manufacturers always include a phone number so that purchasers can call if they have problems putting a product together
    (B) At first, Jimmy was not able to assemble the wagon by himself
    (C) There are several different ways to attach wheels to wagons
    (D) Jimmy has only recently learned how to use his new tool set

12. (A) Some students are more successful if their work is not graded
    (B) The explanation of the grading system in the teacher's handbook is vague
    (C) Some teachers grade more strictly than other teachers
    (D) In order to be fair, a grading system must be agreed upon by both teachers and students

GO ON TO THE NEXT PAGE.

13. (A) No, the weather report predicted thunderstorms the rest of the day
    (B) Yes, the track team practices in all kinds of weather
    (C) No, the skies are clear
    (D) Yes, the rain ended this morning

14. (A) Some topics covered in class are not in the textbook
    (B) Taking notes helps you remember information even if you never look at them again
    (C) The midterm exam tests only the information in the textbook
    (D) Taking notes is a good way to keep from being distracted

15. (A) In order to thrive, certain plants need high humidity, which is hard to maintain in an apartment
    (B) Plants require specific conditions in order to thrive
    (C) All plants should be watered at least once a week, especially if they are grown in containers
    (D) If plants are kept indoors they need more care than if they are allowed to live outside

16. (A) A college-bound student should have strong math skills
    (B) A student must take both math and science to graduate
    (C) A student must have at least three credits in math to graduate
    (D) A student must have at least four credits in math to graduate

17. (A) I'm applying to a graduate program that requires fluency in at least one foreign language
    (B) Some of my classmates are having trouble as well
    (C) Foreign languages are easier to learn the younger you are
    (D) If you learn one romance language, the other romance languages are easier to learn

18. (A) If more women applied for jobs at the company, they would probably be hired
    (B) The jobs available at the company tend to be low-paying
    (C) The number of men working at the company is five times the number of women
    (D) There are three times as many men as women working at the company

19. (A) The problem with the new proposal is that it tries to resolve too many issues at once
    (B) I'm not going to vote in favor of the proposal, even though I think it's a step in the right direction
    (C) Everyone I've talked to agrees that the proposal is too complex for us to make a quick decision
    (D) The woman who submitted the proposal now says she would like to submit some changes to it before a vote is taken

20. (A) Some books take a long time to finish
    (B) I usually read for a few hours after dinner every night
    (C) I think reading is the best way to spend leisure time
    (D) I would rather read than play sports

GO ON TO THE NEXT PAGE.

Part B

<u>Directions:</u> In Part B you will hear six short conversations between two speakers. At the end of each conversation, a third voice will ask questions about what was said. <u>The questions will be spoken just one time.</u> After you hear a conversation and a question about it, read the four possible answers and decide which one would be the best answer to the question. Then, on your answer sheet, find the number of the problem and mark your answer.

EXAMPLE:

You will hear:

You will read: (A) by telephone
(B) by messenger
(C) by letter
(D) by sending a friend to her house

<u>Sample Answer</u>

Ⓐ Ⓑ ● Ⓓ

From the conversation, we know that the man wrote the woman a letter. The best answer, then, is (C), "By letter." Therefore, you should choose answer (C).

Now let us begin Part B. Try to respond to every problem. Be sure to mark all the answers on your answer sheet and completely fill in the lettered space with a heavy, dark mark so that you cannot see the letter.

21. (A) Each of them called the Congresswoman to protest the education bill
(B) Only one of them wrote the Congresswoman to show support for the bill
(C) Neither of them wanted the bill to pass
(D) Both of them gave her neighbors the Congresswoman's address

22. (A) It is more important for students to learn chemistry than to get exercise
(B) Students will not get enough exercise if they are unable to play on school-supported teams
(C) The laboratory equipment necessary for a strong chemistry department is very expensive
(D) The chemistry department is hurt by the funding cut more than the athletic department

23. (A) The speakers agree that the funding cut will affect every department at their school
(B) The first speaker thinks her department is affected the most by the funding cut, because of the high number of students currently playing on sports teams
(C) The second speaker believes that his students will have no alternative means to perform chemistry experiments
(D) Both speakers agree that playing on sports teams and learning chemistry are essential to a student's development

24. (A) at the end of the month
(B) before midterm exams are over
(C) during vacation
(D) next week

GO ON TO THE NEXT PAGE.

25. (A) She is applying to more schools than her classmates are
    (B) She would rather finish her applications than study for midterms
    (C) She has begun writing her essays
    (D) She has finished her essays and is waiting to receive recommendations from her teachers

26. (A) the enlargements
    (B) the color prints
    (C) the color slides
    (D) the film

27. (A) in a week or less
    (B) in about two weeks
    (C) in about three weeks
    (D) before next Thursday

28. (A) She has never run a marathon before
    (B) The marathon in which she hopes to run takes place in six months
    (C) She was not ready for last year's marathon
    (D) She found the first part of her training to be very difficult

29. (A) six months
    (B) between eight months and a year
    (C) a year exactly
    (D) two years

30. (A) arriving after an event has begun
    (B) arriving before an event has begun
    (C) arriving at a pre-arranged meeting time
    (D) arriving before anyone else

31. (A) anger
    (B) cheerfulness
    (C) relief
    (D) optimism

GO ON TO THE NEXT PAGE.

Part C

<u>Directions:</u> In this part of the test, you will hear several short talks. After each talk, you will be asked some questions. <u>The talks and questions will be spoken just one time.</u> They will not be written out for you, so you will have to listen carefully in order to understand and remember what the speaker says.

When you hear a question, read the four possible answers in your test book and decide which one would be the best answer to the question you have heard. Then, on your answer sheet, find the number of the problem and fill in the space that corresponds to the letter of the answer you have chosen.

Now let us begin Part C. Try to respond to every problem. Be sure to mark all answers on your answer sheet and completely fill the lettered space with a heavy, dark mark so that you cannot see the letter.

32. (A) Standardized tests are unfair
(B) Since the quality of education varies so widely in different school districts, standardized tests give some students a marked advantage over others
(C) Because attitude greatly affects performance, standardized test scores may not be accurate measures of knowledge or ability
(D) Before administering a standardized test, a teacher should tell the test-takers that they will get high scores

33. (A) the knowledge the student has learned over time
(B) the quality of teaching at the student's school
(C) the student's emotional state
(D) the psychological development of the student

34. (A) use study guides from a variety of sources so that their preparation will include different points of view
(B) be diligent about their school work starting from the early grades, so that their basic skills will be strong
(C) avoid thinking about the test ahead of time
(D) include confidence-building exercises as part of their preparation for the test

35. (A) whether terminal patients should be able to participate in drug research
(B) whether the testing of drugs for safety is too prolonged
(C) whether the FDA has outlived its usefulness
(D) whether drugs currently being tested will have harmful side effects

36. (A) Critics of the FDA may succeed in limiting the amount of time drugs are tested
(B) The FDA should relax its testing standards for certain cancer drugs
(C) No matter how long the testing lasts, some people will be hurt
(D) Because some drugs have terrible and unforeseen side effects, the FDA rules for testing are appropriate

37. (A) The thalidomide case proved that more extensive testing of new drugs was necessary
(B) Scientists believed that the knowledge gained from longer testing would benefit other areas of research
(C) The lawsuits stemming from unpredicted side effects were costing drug companies millions of dollars a year
(D) The thalidomide case was unusual in that the side effects were not felt by the person actually taking the drug

GO ON TO THE NEXT PAGE.

38. (A) The use of some chemicals in farming is most likely harmless
    (B) Advances in agricultural practices have led to greater crop yields than ever before
    (C) The farming methods of the past are in many ways preferable to modern methods that employ chemicals
    (D) Pesticides cause more damage to water sources than to the soil

39. (A) non-chemical
    (B) healthy
    (C) traditional
    (D) technologically primitive

40. (A) Native Americans
    (B) dairy farmers
    (C) most American farmers
    (D) small farmers

S T O P

THIS IS THE END OF THE LISTENING SECTION.
IF YOU FINISH BEFORE TIME IS CALLED, YOU MAY CHECK YOUR WORK ON THIS SECTION ONLY.
DO NOT WORK ON ANY OTHER SECTION IN THE TEST.

NO TEST MATERIAL ON THIS PAGE.

SECTION 2
READING
Time–30 minutes

<u>Directions</u>: Each statement or passage in this test is followed by a question or questions based on its content. After reading a statement or passage, choose the best answer to each question from among the five choices given. Answer all questions following a statement or passage on the basis of what is <u>stated</u> or <u>implied</u> in that statement or passage. Remember, try to answer every question.

Be sure to mark all your answers on your answer sheet and completely fill in the lettered space with a heavy, dark mark so that you cannot see the letter.

1. Although many students try to get in to the best college they can, some students hesitate to apply to very selective schools because they fear that the academic demands of such a school will be too great. These students should be reassured that the admissions committees will look carefully at their records, and will not offer admission to students who have not demonstrated that they are prepared to handle the work load.

    According to the statement, a student who has been accepted for admission to a very selective college

    (A) would be wise to apply to more than one college or university
    (B) should take courses during the summer in any subjects in which she did not excel
    (C) should take only the least demanding courses during the first semester of college
    (D) should not attend that college unless she has taken advanced courses in high school
    (E) should feel confident that she will be ready to do the required work

Questions 2-3 refer to the following passage.

In a traditional classroom, subjects are usually taught one at a time during a specified period each day, and the school day is divided into periods of equal length. Currently, however, some schools have instituted an integrated teaching plan, in which subjects are not separated into rigid time slots, but taught together in various combinations. The integrated teaching plan particularly benefits the student who has trouble with a particular subject, since the student does not have to endure an hour or so devoted entirely to that subject. Also, the fact that the subject is taught in conjunction with one or more other subjects may make the troublesome subject easier to learn.

2. Which of the following is the best example of what might take place in a classroom where an integrated teaching plan is used?

    (A) Students are given a quiz on last night's homework, and then asked to grade each other's work
    (B) The teacher gives a lecture on Shakespeare, and the students then act out selected parts of one of his plays
    (C) The teacher divides the class into small discussion groups, and gives each group a short story to read and report on
    (D) Students are allowed to progress through their math workbooks at their own pace, with the teacher available during class to answer questions
    (E) Students are given art materials so that they can make a mural depicting an important moment in history

GO ON TO THE NEXT PAGE.

3. The passage supplies information for answering which of the following questions?

    (A) How were integrated teaching plans developed?
    (B) Are integrated teaching plans currently more popular than traditional teaching plans?
    (C) How does an integrated teaching plan help a student who finds a certain subject difficult?
    (D) Do gifted students respond as well to integrated teaching plans as do students with academic difficulties?
    (E) Do some schools use integrated teaching plans for some subjects and not others?

4. Reginald is the best basketball player this school has ever had; after all, he holds the record for the most points scored in one game.

    The author of the statement assumes which of the following?

    (A) Reginald will probably not beat his own record this year
    (B) Performance in a single game is the best measure of a basketball player
    (C) Great basketball players consistently score a lot of points per game
    (D) Some local basketball players are better than Reginald, but they play for other teams
    (E) Reginald almost always rebounds as well as he shoots

Questions 5-6 refer to the following passage.

Traditionally, schools are biased toward verbal skills, valuing written and spoken expression over everything else. Yet some of us naturally excel in math, or quantitative skills, rather than language; still others may be best at spatial logic, or dealing with shapes and how they behave in space. Although verbal skills are important, teachers must find ways not only to avoid demanding the same level of such skills from every student, but also to exploit the other skills a student may possess.

5. The author's primary purpose is to

    (A) argue that verbal skills are not as important as other skills
    (B) assert that the more skills a person has, the easier learning will be
    (C) point out that people have different strengths that should not be ignored
    (D) demand that teachers keep their classrooms free from all kinds of bias
    (E) question whether quantitative skills are actually useful

6. A person who has strong spatial skills would most likely excel at which of the following tasks?

    (A) Devising an original card game
    (B) Designing a mobile
    (C) Analyzing the meter and rhyme of a poem
    (D) Solving a series of algebraic equations
    (E) Writing a simple computer program

GO ON TO THE NEXT PAGE.

7. To satisfy the physical education requirement, students may choose gymnastics, basketball, football, or field hockey for the first semester, and soccer, track, basketball, or calisthenics for the second semester. Basketball, gymnastics, and calisthenics are indoor sports; a student may not take indoor sports for both semesters.

If a student takes basketball for the first semester, which of the following sports would satisfy the requirement for the second semester?

   I. Soccer, calisthenics, or track
   II. Soccer, field hockey, or track
   III. Soccer or track

(A) I only
(B) II only
(C) III only
(D) I and II only
(E) II and III only

Questions 8-10 refer to the following passage.

Some have argued that Hollywood is to blame for wasting some of this country's finest literary talent. It is true that the lure of large sums of money proved too tempting to resist for F. Scott Fitzgerald, William Faulkner, and others. However, it is not certain that if they had resisted, they would have produced more literary masterworks. Possibly the quick money they earned in Hollywood, as well as having to write under short deadlines and within a specific structure, was helpful to their literary work. And if a literary writer failed to produce anything of substance after working in Hollywood, perhaps Hollywood had nothing to do with that failure.

8. The primary purpose of the passage is to

(A) give a short history of the connection between literature and the movies
(B) explain the ways in which working in Hollywood can aid the development of a writer
(C) lament the fact that literary writers must sometimes work simply for financial reasons
(D) argue that working in Hollywood was not necessarily detrimental to literary authors
(E) discuss the effects of working in the movie business

9. The author of the passage would probably DISAGREE with which of the following statements?

(A) F. Scott Fitzgerald and William Faulkner are both great literary talents
(B) Movies will always be more popular than books
(C) Hollywood cannot be blamed for the failure of some writers to produce literary masterworks after working there
(D) Having to write within certain constraints can be good for a writer's development
(E) If a writer has serious literary aspirations, he should not work in any other medium

10. The passage supplies information for answering which of the following questions?

(A) Were the movies written by Fitzgerald and Faulkner successful?
(B) Were Fitzgerald and Faulkner the only literary writers to work in Hollywood?
(C) Did Fitzgerald and Faulkner make money from their books?
(D) At what point in their careers did Fitzgerald and Faulkner work in Hollywood?
(E) Why did Fitzgerald and Faulkner choose to work in Hollywood rather than find another way to make money?

GO ON TO THE NEXT PAGE.

11. A recent study of college-bound high school students found that a high percentage of these students had at least one parent who had been to college; for those students, it seems that going to college was something they had been expected to do from an early age and did not involve their making a conscious choice to do so.

    Which of the following inferences can be drawn from the statement above?

    (A) If a student does not make a conscious choice to go to college, his performance will be average at best

    (B) High schools should make more of an effort to encourage their students to go to college

    (C) Once in college, students whose parents did not go to college outperform students who had at least one parent who went to college

    (D) College-bound students whose parents did not go to college make an active decision to attend college

    (E) The decision to go to college is made by parents, not students

Questions 12-13 refer to the following passage.

Through the "1950s," high school classrooms were strictly run, and students punished for small infractions; more importantly, students were expected to attain some level of competence in such academic subjects as Latin and trigonometry. During the "1960s" and "1970s," however, what was expected of students in both academics and behavior changed rather dramatically. In many schools, students were allowed to smoke, and punishments for misbehavior were minimal. The course work required became "soft," allowing large numbers of students to graduate after only taking enough math to balance a checkbook. In the "1990s," this unhappy trend has been challenged, at least to some degree. Principals of some large urban high schools have demanded that their students adhere to a strict behavioral code, as well as complete more rigorous courses. Having high expectations for students is really the only way to assure them that they are capable of achievement.

12. The author of the passage would most likely DISAPPROVE of which of the following?

    (A) A physics course in which the students build a small bridge on campus

    (B) A first-year Latin course required for all students

    (C) A Spanish course that requires students to eat lunch together every day so they can practice speaking Spanish informally

    (D) A history course in which students write a thirty-page term paper

    (E) An English course that spends two months studying comic books

GO ON TO THE NEXT PAGE.

13. The author would most likely agree with which of the following statements?

    (A) "Soft" math classes are never appropriate for any students

    (B) Achievement is best promoted by adapting the curriculum to the individual student's needs

    (C) If little is demanded of students, they will be unlikely to achieve very much

    (D) Latin should still be a required course for all high school students

    (E) Behavior problems endanger the success of high schools more than do minimal course requirements

14. Since the county refuses to consider a tax increase, it is certain that next year we will not have adequate funding for our schools.

    The author of the statement makes which of the following assumptions?

    (A) The only way that the county schools will have adequate funding is through a tax increase

    (B) County officials are unconcerned about education

    (C) Tax increases do not always benefit county schools

    (D) "Adequate funding" means having only enough money to meet payroll, pay for building maintenance, and cover basic after-school activities

    (E) The county schools were inadequately funded this year

Questions 15-19 refer to the following passage.

American schools have come under serious criticism in recent years, due in part to falling test scores and to studies documenting that many students graduate from high school lacking basic
(5) knowledge. But what is even more troubling is that many students who perform well in school may not have gained a real understanding of the course material. Further studies have shown that when the format or wording of test questions is altered
(10) slightly, these "good" students fail to answer the questions correctly.

Part of the problem, as some have suggested, lies with the emphasis schools place on test performance, and in the very way the tests are con-
(15) structed. If test questions ask only that students repeat back what has been said in class, they have no chance to demonstrate that they actually understand what they have been taught.

If a history class has been studying revolutions,
(20) for example, the usual testing method is to ask specifically about those revolutions covered in class. The test results, therefore, will show how well a student can memorize facts, not how well he can use those facts conceptually. A better testing
(25) method might be to ask students to use what they have learned in class to analyze and draw conclusions about a contemporary revolution, which would allow the students to show their mastery (or lack of it) of the material. It is important to remem-
(30) ber that knowing facts is only the first step to understanding; the ultimate goal is to be able to use those facts to solve problems and to reach a full appreciation of the subject.

GO ON TO THE NEXT PAGE.

15. What is the main idea of the passage?

    (A) Essay questions are better than multiple-choice questions at measuring a student's proficiency
    (B) The ways in which schools test students do not adequately measure whether the students have a true grasp of the material
    (C) The fact that many students graduate without basic knowledge is a bigger problem than the fact that students who perform well may not thoroughly understand what they have studied
    (D) Factual knowledge is a crucial step in gaining true understanding
    (E) If new methods of testing show that students do not understand the material, the teacher should adopt a different teaching approach

16. The author encloses the word "good" (line 10) in quotation marks in order to

    (A) indicate irony
    (B) emphasize approval
    (C) show disinterest
    (D) show that the word was spoken by someone else
    (E) demonstrate enthusiasm

17. The author asserts that which of the following is (are) partly to blame for the failure of students to understand course material?

    I. Schools value test scores more than they should
    II. Test questions do not challenge students to use their factual knowledge
    III. Students graduate from high school without fundamental knowledge

    (A) I only
    (B) II only
    (C) I and II only
    (D) II and III only
    (E) I, II, and III

18. The author of the passage would most likely approve of which of the following testing methods for a class that has been studying chemistry?

    (A) Students are given a list of the elements and a list of abbreviations and asked to match them correctly
    (B) Students are given problems to solve that are very similar to the examples in the textbook
    (C) Students are asked to describe the steps of an experiment performed earlier in class
    (D) For a series of chemical terms, students are given five definitions and asked to choose the appropriate one
    (E) Students are given an unfamiliar material to experiment with and asked to describe some of its chemical properties

19. According to the passage, which of the following will result if a student learns the facts but does not understand the subject?

    (A) She will not be able to take more advanced courses in that subject
    (B) She will not succeed academically
    (C) She will develop an acceptable capacity for memorization
    (D) She will be unable to use those facts to solve problems
    (E) She will develop a greater appreciation for the complexity of the subject

GO ON TO THE NEXT PAGE.

20. In 1870, less than one percent of the population attended college; a hundred years later, the figure was greater than forty percent. This tremendous change has more to do with the job market than with any dramatic increase in people's thirst for knowledge.

    Which of the following is the most accurate inference that can be drawn from the statements above?

    (A) A person now has a better chance of getting a good job with a college education
    (B) Before the 1970s, most people could not afford to go to college
    (C) Those who went to college in the nineteenth century did not do so for professional reasons
    (D) A nineteenth-century college education did little to prepare students for the real world
    (E) Many jobs currently require technical expertise

Questions 21-22 refer to the following passage.

One of the mistakes students make when taking standardized tests is that they work too quickly on easy questions and spend too much time on difficult questions. It's understandable that this should happen, because on many regular course-work tests, more points are awarded for difficult questions. On most standardized tests, however, difficult questions and easy questions are worth the same number of points.

21. The author suggests that it's a mistake for a student to work too quickly on an easy standardized test question for which of the following reasons?

    (A) When taking a standardized test, students should work at a consistent pace throughout
    (B) Since an easy and difficult question have equal point value, it makes sense to spend more time on those questions a student is likely to get right
    (C) Easy questions are actually worth more points than difficult questions
    (D) Although standardized tests often cover subjects learned in school, good strategies for taking such tests are usually not taught
    (E) Students who are able to get difficult questions correct should not make careless errors

22. Which of the following inferences can be most reasonably drawn from the statements above?

    (A) Students with high grades usually perform less well on standardized tests
    (B) Teachers should only give standardized tests so that students will know what to expect
    (C) The scoring system for standardized tests is unfair
    (D) A good strategy for taking a test on regular course work is not necessarily a good strategy for taking a standardized test
    (E) If a student does poorly on a standardized test, it is because the student worked at the wrong speed

GO ON TO THE NEXT PAGE.

23. If athletes do not eat nutritious food and get enough sleep in the week before a competition, they should not expect to perform well.

   Which of the following is the most accurate inference that can be drawn from the statement above?

   (A) Very talented athletes will perform well whether or not they have eaten well and gotten enough sleep

   (B) Athletes who rarely eat well or get enough sleep usually perform well because they are used to competing under adverse conditions

   (C) Athletes who eat well and get enough sleep will outperform athletes who did not

   (D) Athletes who eat well and get enough sleep have a better chance of doing their best in a competition than athletes who do not

   (E) If athletes truly want to win, they will eat well, get enough sleep, and practice hard

Questions 24-29 refer to the following passage.

   Because the Constitution said nothing about education, during the end of the eighteenth century education was left up to the states and individual towns. The biggest issue at that time was making (5) some minimum amount of education compulsory, although even the states that passed such laws intended them to apply only to whites. Finally, in 1865, a federal bureau began to develop black schools, and land grants were set aside for the (10) formation of black colleges. Since that time, the federal government—including the courts—has become increasingly involved with education, white and black, from pre-school all the way to graduate school.

   (15) In 1896, the Supreme Court ruled in the infamous *Plessy v. Ferguson* that public schools could be "separate but equal", a ruling that severely limited educational opportunities for blacks. Not until 1954, with the Court's *Brown v. Board of Education*, (20) was racial segregation in schools no longer sanctioned by the federal government.

   In later decades, both the states and federal government sponsored programs aimed at providing education to disadvantaged children, and (25) instituted forced busing in an attempt to fix some of the problems caused by years of segregation. Yet the success of government in providing education to all citizens remains mixed, at best; state and federal government, along with teachers, administrators, and parents, continue to battle for control of (30) public schools, often to the detriment of the students themselves.

24. The author's primary purpose is to

   (A) criticize the Supreme Court for its rulings on education

   (B) prove that the reason educational opportunities for blacks were limited was that the states did not act responsibly

   (C) argue that education should have been mandatory for all children

   (D) show that government intervention in public education has not been entirely positive

   (E) explain why *Plessy v. Ferguson* was such a setback to black education

GO ON TO THE NEXT PAGE.

25. The author describes *Plessy v. Ferguson* as "infamous" (lines 15-16) in order to

   (A) point out that the Supreme Court knew that it was making history
   (B) acknowledge that the decision is familiar to most people
   (C) characterize the decision as being known for its negative effect
   (D) question whether the Supreme Court understood the ramifications of the decision
   (E) imply that too few people know about the decision

26. The author implies that the role of the federal government in education has not been clear because

   (A) the Supreme Court has historically made conflicting rulings on education
   (B) the states have never willingly ceded control over education to the federal government
   (C) the federal government has only been involved in education in the last few decades
   (D) the Constitution failed to include education as one of the government's duties
   (E) parents have always preferred that public schools not be regulated by the government

27. The passage would most likely be found in which of the following?

   (A) A book advocating educational reform
   (B) A pamphlet for new public school teachers
   (C) A textbook for high school history students
   (D) A world history textbook
   (E) A book about the legislative branch of the federal government

28. The author mentions land grants as an example of which of the following?

   (A) One of the first efforts by the federal government to provide education for blacks
   (B) A typical battle for control between the states and the federal government
   (C) A result of a provision of the Constitution that guarantees education for all citizens
   (D) An early attempt by civil-rights workers to create new educational opportunities
   (E) A result stemming from voters demanding action from Congress

GO ON TO THE NEXT PAGE.

29. The author would most likely agree with which of the following statements about the role of government in education?

   (A) Education should be controlled by parents and local governments

   (B) Students should have an active voice in planning their education

   (C) The government should be responsible for making sure that all children have access to education

   (D) Because the government has made some mistakes in the past, it should not be involved in making education policy today

   (E) Decisions about educational policy should be left to Congress, not the courts

30. Dora: For our class project, we are making a model of Monticello, which was built by Thomas Jefferson.

   Robert: Jefferson is one of the most interesting presidents, because he was an architect, a gardener, and an inventor, as well as a politician.

   Dora: We will most likely raise enough money this semester for the whole class to take a field trip to Monticello.

   Robert: That's a long way to travel, but I guess you will learn a lot.

   If neither of the speakers is making false statements, which of the following is an accurate description of the conversation?

   (A) Dora states only opinions in both of her statements

   (B) Dora states opinion in her first statement, and fact in her second statement

   (C) Robert and Dora both state opinion and fact

   (D) Robert and Dora state only facts in their first statements

   (E) Robert states only opinion in his first statement

STOP

THIS IS THE END OF THE READING SECTION.
IF YOU FINISH BEFORE TIME IS CALLED, YOU MAY CHECK YOUR WORK ON THIS SECTION ONLY.
DO NOT WORK ON ANY OTHER SECTION IN THE TEST.

SECTION 3
WRITING
Time–30 minutes
Part A
(Suggested time–10 minutes)

Directions: In each of the sentences below four portions are underlined and lettered. Read each sentence and decide whether any of the underlined parts contain a grammatical construction, a word use, or an instance of incorrect or omitted punctuation that would be inappropriate in carefully written English. If so, note the letter printed beneath the underlined portion and completely fill in the corresponding lettered space on the answer sheet with a heavy, dark mark so that you cannot see the letter.

If there are no errors in any of the underlined portions, fill in space E. No sentence has more than one error. Remember, try to answer every question.

EXAMPLES:

1. He spoke <u>bluntly</u> and <u>angrily</u> to <u>we</u> <u>spectators</u>.
             A   B   C   D

    <u>No error</u>
      E

2. Margaret <u>insists</u> <u>that</u> these books ⌐ flowers,
               A   B   C

    and dolls ⌐ are hers. <u>no error</u>
          D   E

1. The editors <u>were more worried</u> about the
                        A

    decrease in state funding for the arts <u>as</u> about
                                             B

    the rise in postage costs <u>that could mean</u> <u>fewer</u>
                                      C   D

    submissions to their magazine. <u>No error</u>
                                          E

2. Concerned that diplomatic plans had

    <u>gone awry</u>, the officials prepared to make a
        A

    quick trip to the capital of <u>North Korea</u>,
                                        B

    <u>leaving an assistant</u> in charge of the office in
            C

    <u>their</u> absence. <u>No error</u>
       D   E

3. Followers of Rachel Carson believe that

    <u>those who promote</u> the manufacture and
            A

    <u>use of</u> pesticides and herbicides <u>makes</u> a
       B   C

    grave error; Carson's *The Silent Spring*

    <u>describes</u> the irreparable harm such products
        D

    do to the environment. <u>No error</u>
                                  E

GO ON TO THE NEXT PAGE.

4. While criticizing television for providing
      A   B

   hours of mindless entertainment, the

   committee surprisingly praised the networks

   for creating a few innovative dramas that are
                        C

   as good as anything showing in movie
     D

   theaters. No error
          E

5. The McCarthy hearings were the impetus

   for the creation of the infamous blacklist,
       A

   which contained those who had attended
               B

   Communist Party meetings or

   were suspected of having the slightest
      C

   sympathy with Communist ideas. No error
     D   E

6. Although the school board is resisting the
                     A

   institution of yet another new curriculum, the

   members unanimously agree that its time to
           B   C

   change the hierarchy in the administration,

   which has been called outdated and overly
      D

   rigid. No error
      E

7. What became clear in the 1980s was that
     A

   women were finding it difficult to raise their

   families and concentrate on their careers at
           B

   the same time; the demands of the office, as
                         C

   well as those of their children and husbands,
     D

   left these career women without any time for

   themselves. No error
           E

8. When the farmer posted "No Trespassing"

   signs warning that deer hunting was not
      A

   allowed on his property, he was not making
                    B

   an idle threat; he fully intended to persecute
           C   D

   anyone violating the law. No error
          E

9. Americans have been abusing the miraculous
           A

   antibiotics almost from the minute they
                  B

   were discovered, with the result that bacteria
     C

   have mutated to form resistant strains

   that are unaffected by the formerly powerful
          D

   medicines. No error
          E

GO ON TO THE NEXT PAGE.

10. Also developed during the nineteenth century

    the long-blooming floribunda rose, as well as
        A

    the hybrid tea rose, are known for the perfect
                              B

    shape of its blossoms which grow on long
             C   D

    stems. No error
          E

11. Although the planning committee meeting

    had lasted for six hours, the members
     A

    were unable to come to a consensus of opinion
      B   C

    on whether to spend the grant money on a
       D

    new playground or on building renovations.

    No error
     E

12. Because Vincent Van Gogh, like Claude
                             A

    Monet, is known for his beautiful paintings of
          B

    landscapes and flowers, their work is
                            C

    widely reproduced and can be found on
         D

    posters everywhere. No error
                         E

13. Johnson finally left the sporting goods store
            A

    empty-handed; he was unable to decide
                 B   C

    between a rugged mountain bike or a racing
                                 D

    bike that only weighed seven pounds.

    No error
     E

14. Left to his own devices, Peter
        A

    would have traveled with more suitcases and
        B

    trunks than three porters could carry, because
                                         C

    he had a terrible fear of finding himself in a
                           D

    new place without the proper clothes.

    No error
     E

15. Even though cholesterol levels appear to be an
     A   B

    inherited trait, they can be lowered through a
                     C

    program of diet, medication, and

    getting regular exercise. No error
         D   E

16. The Nobel Prize-winning chemist

    succeeding by concentrating on a very narrow
         A

    problem; his genius did not spring from wide-
                        B

    ranging knowledge but from his ability to
                       C

    rebuff all distractions for over thirty years.
                            D

    No error
     E

17. Now that vaccines are easily available to even
     A   B

    the poorest citizens, there is not any longer an
                              C   D

    excuse for outbreaks of polio or smallpox.

    No error
     E

GO ON TO THE NEXT PAGE.

18. His mother <u>was amazed</u> that Jeffrey was
                     A

    <u>so skinny</u>, since his diet was limited <u>to such</u>
        B   C

    calorie-laden foods <u>like</u> onion rings, potato
                          D

    chips, and hamburgers. <u>No error</u>
                              E

19. When the play finally opens next month in

    the newly renovated theater, the audience

    <u>would be delighted</u> to see that the interior is
        A

    as beautiful and ornate <u>as it was</u> when the
                                B

    theater was built in 1850, and that the stage

    <u>itself</u> has been designed <u>to accommodate</u> a
        C   D

    large number of modern special effects.

        <u>No error</u>
           E

20. Designed partly to satisfy stricter laws

    applying to the auto industry, and <u>costing</u>
                                          A

    many millions to develop, the electric cars

    currently available from <u>at</u> <u>least one</u> American
                                B   C

    manufacturer can be driven almost <u>as quick as</u>
                                          D

    some gas-powered compact cars.   <u>No error</u>
                                        E

21. The land has tremendous meaning

    <u>to the Navajo</u>, both <u>because of its</u> religious
        A   B

    significance and because <u>the tribe has</u>
                                C

    traditionally used <u>it</u> to support large flocks of
                          D

    sheep. <u>No error</u>
               E

22. If the cancer-causing asbestos in the ceiling

    <u>would not have</u> been partially <u>decayed</u>, it
        A   B

    would not have posed <u>such</u> an immediate
                            C

    health hazard <u>to</u> the students in the
                     D

    classroom. <u>No error</u>
                   E

23. <u>To businessmen</u> in the United States, China
        A

    represents a vast and virtually untapped

    market; <u>thus</u>, the problem of <u>how</u> to distribute
               B   C

    products in a country where transportation is

    difficult at best has <u>yet to be solved</u>. <u>No error</u>
                             D   E

GO ON TO THE NEXT PAGE.

24. A bomb shelter <u>capable of</u> protecting <u>its</u>
                    A   B

inhabitants from nuclear fallout would not

only have to be at least four feet thick,

<u>but also</u> provide shelter for three to five years,
    C

<u>the length of time</u> it takes for the fallout to
            D

settle. <u>No error</u>
            E

25. The parents of the teenager were horrified <u>to</u>
                                                   A

find out <u>how</u> their son <u>had</u> <u>been sneaking</u>
          B   C   D

undetected out of the house at night by

climbing down the fire escape. <u>No error</u>
                                   E

GO ON TO THE NEXT PAGE.

Part B

(Suggested time–10 minutes)

Directions: In each of the following sentences some part of the sentence or the entire sentence is underlined. The underlined part presents a problem in the appropriate use of language. Beneath each sentence you will find five ways of writing the underlined part. The first of these repeats the original, but the other four are all different. If you think the original sentence is better than any of the suggested changes, you should choose answer A; otherwise you should mark one of the other choices. Select the best answer and completely fill in the corresponding lettered space on the answer sheet with a heavy, dark mark so that you cannot see the letter.

This is a test of correctness and effectiveness of expression. In choosing answers, follow the requirements of standard written English; that is, pay attention to acceptable usage in grammar, diction (choice of words), sentence construction, and punctuation. Choose the answer that produces the most effective sentence—clear and exact, without awkwardness or ambiguity. Do not make a choice that changes the meaning of the original sentence.

EXAMPLES:

Sample Answer

1. <u>While waving</u> goodbye to our friends, the airplane took off, and we watched it disappear in the sky.

   1. Ⓐ Ⓑ ● Ⓓ Ⓔ

  (A)   While waving
  (B)   Waving
  (C)   As we were waving
  (D)   While we are waving
  (E)   During waving

Sample Answer

2. Modern travelers seem to prefer speed <u>to comfort</u>.

   2. ● Ⓑ Ⓒ Ⓓ Ⓔ

  (A)   to comfort
  (B)   than comfort
  (C)   rather than being comfortable
  (D)   instead of being comfortable
  (E)   more than comfort

26. The trip to Paris was only <u>the second time Mary vacations away from home</u>.

  (A)   the second time Mary vacations away from home
  (B)   the second time in which Mary was vacationing away from home
  (C)   Mary's second time when she was vacationing away from home
  (D)   Mary's second vacation away from home
  (E)   Mary's second vacationing away from home

27. When the dam broke, the rush of water was <u>such a power</u> that cars and houses were swept downstream.

  (A)   such a power
  (B)   of so much power
  (C)   such powerful
  (D)   so powerful
  (E)   so much power

GO ON TO THE NEXT PAGE.

28. <u>Having over the years been raising hundreds of cows, nevertheless he lost four calves</u> during the month-long cold spell.

   (A) Having over the years been raising hundreds of cows, nevertheless he lost four calves
   (B) Over the years he has raised hundreds of cows, and nevertheless he lost four calves
   (C) Even though he has raised hundreds of cows over the years, he nevertheless lost four calves
   (D) Having raised hundreds of cows over the years, four calves were lost nevertheless
   (E) Despite raising hundreds of cows over the years, he lost four cows nevertheless

29. According to the professor, a good student is defined <u>as one who is</u> attentive in class, reviews her notes after class, and does extra reading whether she will be tested on it or not.

   (A) as one who is
   (B) as the one being
   (C) as those who are
   (D) to be
   (E) to be one who

30. <u>At what point in time</u> will the report be ready for publication?

   (A) At what point in time
   (B) At which time
   (C) On which date and time
   (D) On what date and time
   (E) When

31. Warning that this country's farmland is not in good health, agriculturists name soil erosion as the top danger, followed by overgrazing, compaction, and <u>the way pesticides and chemical fertilizers are used</u>.

   (A) the way pesticides and fertilizers are used
   (B) how pesticides and fertilizers are being used
   (C) the using of pesticides as well as chemical fertilizers
   (D) the use of pesticides and chemical fertilizers
   (E) pesticides and chemical fertilizer being used

32. When it appeared to Richard Nixon that impeachment proceedings were unavoidable, <u>the presidency was resigned by him even though</u> many of his supporters wanted to continue to fight the opposition.

   (A) the presidency was resigned by him even though
   (B) he resigned as president even though
   (C) he made his resignation of the presidency, since
   (D) the presidency he then resigned, but
   (E) he resigned the presidency, despite

33. Attempting to resolve the issue of building a bike lane through the center of <u>town, it was discussed by the transportation committee</u> whether the lane would be used by enough people to justify the expense

   (A) town, it was discussed by the transportation committee
   (B) town; it was discussed by the transportation committee
   (C) town, discussion by the transportation committee about
   (D) town, the transportation committee discussed
   (E) town; the transportation committee was discussing

GO ON TO THE NEXT PAGE.

34. If you have any hope of passing the upcoming math <u>test, you must try to spend</u> a few hours each night practicing your new skills.

    (A)   test, you must try to spend
    (B)   test, you must try and spend
    (C)   test you should try to be spending
    (D)   test; try to spend
    (E)   test, trying to spend

35. Believing the problem to be one of "bad habits," for years doctors have tried to help the obese <u>through recommendations of a low-fat diet, getting plenty of exercise, and using behavior modification</u>; however, new research suggests that the cause of obesity may be largely genetic.

    (A)   through recommendations of a low-fat diet, getting plenty of exercise, and using behavior modification
    (B)   with a recommendation of a diet low in fat, plenty of exercise, and the use of behavior modification
    (C)   by the recommending of a low-fat diet, plenty of exercise, and of behavior modification
    (D)   by recommending they follow a low-fat diet, plenty of exercise, and behavior modification
    (E)   by recommending a low-fat diet, plenty of exercise, and behavior modification

GO ON TO THE NEXT PAGE.

Part C
(Suggested time–10 minutes)

<u>Directions:</u> Each of the questions or incomplete statements below is followed by five suggested answers or completions. Select the one that is best in each case and completely fill in the corresponding lettered space on the answer sheet with a heavy, dark mark so that you cannot see the letter.

Remember, try to answer every question.

<u>Question 36</u> is based on the following.

It is incomprehensible that the Congress is allowing the Clean Air Act to be dismantled and weakened beyond recognition. Since its passage in 1970, the air quality in much of the country had slowly begun to improve—but there is little hope now that these gains will remain, much less that we will see further improvement.

36. The tone of the passage above can best be described as

(A) conciliatory
(B) apathetic
(C) dogmatic
(D) angry
(E) enthusiastic

37. Which of the following statements can be described as opinion rather than fact?

(A) Cubism, a painting style developed in the 20th century, is characterized by geometric forms and limited colors
(B) The subject matter of cubist paintings is usually still life or occasionally portraits
(C) Rather than using traditional techniques of perspective, cubist artists created the illusion of depth by painting overlapping planes
(D) Cubism was developed as a reaction to the very different Impressionist and Romantic styles that came before it
(E) Picasso's *Les Desmoiselles d'Avignon* is not only one of the best examples of cubism, but one of the first to be created

<u>Questions 38-41</u> are based on the following.

(1) Viruses are surprisingly successful organisms, considering they cannot perform any life functions by themselves. (2) Consisting primarily of DNA or RNA, they enter a host cell and take it over, using the cell to produce more viruses. (3) This destroys the cell, causing diseases such as polio, influenza, and smallpox.
(4) The immune system of the body fights viruses by producing antibodies that prevent the virus from attacking. (5) Currently, _____ , synthetic vaccines are available that pose no risk of infection from the virus. (6) Since antibodies are only manufactured as a result of exposure to a virus, scientists first injected people with small amounts of killed virus to stimulate the production of antibodies. (7) _____.

38. The passage would make better sense if which two sentences were reversed?

(A) 1 and 2
(B) 2 and 3
(C) 3 and 4
(D) 4 and 5
(E) 5 and 6

GO ON TO THE NEXT PAGE.

39. Which of the following is the best revision of sentence 3?

    (A) This reproduction, destroying the cell, causes a variety of diseases such as polio, influenza, and smallpox

    (B) The reproductive process both destroys the cell and is the cause of a number of diseases, examples of which are polio, influenza, or smallpox

    (C) The process of viral reproduction destroys the cell and causes diseases such as polio, influenza or smallpox

    (D) Polio, influenza, and smallpox are all examples of the types of diseases that are caused when the process of viral reproduction destroys the cell

    (E) Polio, influenza, and smallpox are the result of the cell's destruction during the viral process of reproduction

40. Which of the following best completes sentence 5?

    (A) however
    (B) nonetheless
    (C) therefore
    (D) notwithstanding
    (E) moreover

41. Which of the following is the most appropriate choice for sentence 7?

    (A) When vaccines were first developed, some patients responded by becoming ill rather than producing antibodies

    (B) Jonas Salk developed the polio vaccine in 1952

    (C) Unlike viruses, bacteria are responsive to antibiotic drugs, although the effectiveness of these drugs has diminished due to overuse

    (D) Although vaccines have virtually eliminated the spread of some viruses, the amazingly adaptive organisms continue to evolve; it is hard to imagine we will ever live in a world altogether free from viral infection

    (E) If an unvaccinated person is infected with the polio virus, he may become paralyzed from the effect of the virus on the nervous system, or he may produce enough antibodies to recover

42. The use of landfills as a solution for this country's waste problem is no longer workable.

    The answer to which of the following questions would be LEAST useful as evidence to support the statement above?

    (A) How long will existing landfills will be able to accommodate more waste?

    (B) How many tons of waste are produced in the country each day?

    (C) What are the environmental problems caused by existing landfills?

    (D) Have some communities implemented recycling programs?

    (E) Do safe alternatives to landfills exist?

GO ON TO THE NEXT PAGE.

Questions 43-44

If the President, by declaring war, is called a hawk, then the electorate may fairly be termed ostriches. And rather than exert any reason on the situation, members of Congress run around Washington like chickens with their heads cut off. It is difficult to maintain even the appearance of optimism, since_____.

43. The author uses the word "ostriches" to imply that the electorate

   (A) is acting silly
   (B) is avoiding reality
   (C) is in favor of peace
   (D) supports the decisions of the President
   (E) reaches its conclusions only after thorough consideration of the facts

44. Which of the following best completes the final sentence and continues the metaphor of the passage?

   (A) war will only result in the needless death of our nation's youth
   (B) waging a war successfully is more difficult than scaling the most treacherous mountain peak, and this President is not known for his physical stamina
   (C) the tide seems to have turned; our leaders are content to float along the current of emotion instead of keeping their feet on the ground
   (D) from the President's first days in office, he has kept himself in the dark and allowed his advisers to steer the boat
   (E) the days of foreign policy owls such as Thomas Jefferson and Franklin Roosevelt appear to have gone the way of the dodo

45. (1) Theater is by nature an ephemeral event, unlike novels and poetry; once a performance is over, it's gone, and the next night's performance will in some way be different. (2) Sometimes the play itself doesn't have long life, while others—like Shakespeare's—are performed over and over, throughout the world. (3) Theater first began as primitive peoples invented dances that dramatized scenes of hunting and battle. (4) Perhaps the fleeting quality of theater is part of its attraction, because to be a part of the company, or the audience, is to experience something that cannot be repeated.

   Which sentence interrupts the flow of the passage?

   (A) 1
   (B) 2
   (C) 3
   (D) 4
   (E) None of the above

S T O P

THIS IS THE END OF THE WRITING SECTION.
IF YOU FINISH BEFORE TIME IS CALLED, YOU MAY CHECK YOUR WORK ON THIS SECTION ONLY.
DO NOT WORK ON ANY OTHER SECTION IN THE TEST.

NO TEST MATERIAL ON THIS PAGE.

SECTION 4
ESSAY
Time–30 minutes

Your local school board is scheduled to vote on whether teachers and administrators should be allowed to use corporal punishment, or "paddling," as a disciplinary tool. Write a letter to the editor of the local paper explaining whether you support corporal punishment and give specific reasons for your position.

GO ON TO THE NEXT PAGE.

S T O P

THIS IS THE END OF THE ESSAY SECTION.
IF YOU FINISH BEFORE TIME IS CALLED, YOU MAY CHECK YOUR WORK ON THIS SECTION ONLY.
DO NOT WORK ON ANY OTHER SECTION IN THE TEST.

NO TEST MATERIAL ON THIS PAGE.

Core Battery: Test of Professional Knowledge

This test book is divided into four separate sections. You will find a time limit printed at the beginning of each of the four sections. During the time indicated, you are to work on that section only. The supervisor will tell you when to begin and when to end each section. If you finish a section before time is called, you may check your work on that section, but you may not work on any of the other sections.

Work as rapidly as you can without sacrificing accuracy. Do not spend too much time puzzling over a question that seems too difficult for you. Answer the easier questions first; then return to the harder ones. Try to answer every question even if you have to guess. Your score will be based on the number of questions you answer correctly. Unanswered questions will be counted in the same way as wrong answers.

Where necessary, you may use blank spaces in the test book for scratch paper. Do not use any other paper or the margins or back of the answer sheet to do scratchwork.

YOU MUST INDICATE ALL OF YOUR ANSWERS ON THE SEPARATE ANSWER SHEET. No credit will be given for anything written in this test book. Afetr you have decided which of the suggested answers is best, fill in the corresponding lettered space on the answer sheet. BE SURE THAT EACH MARK IS HEAVY AND DARK AND COMPLETELY FILLS THE ANSWER SPACE. Light or partial marks may not be read by the scoring machine.

EXAMPLE:

Sample Answer

Which of the following is the capital of the United States?

(A) New York, NY
(B) Washington, DC
(C) Chicago, IL
(D) Los Angeles, CA
(E) Boston, MA

Give only one answer to each question. If you change an answer, be sure that the previous mark is erased completely. Incomplete erasures may be read as intended answers.

Time Limits

SECTION 1	30 minutes
SECTION 2	30 minutes
SECTION 3	30 minutes
SECTION 4	30 minutes
Total	120 minutes

SECTION 1
Time–30 minutes

<u>Directions</u>: Each of the questions or incomplete statements below is followed by five suggested answers or completions. Select the one that is best in each case and then fill in the corresponding lettered space on the answer sheet with a heavy, dark mark so that you cannot see the letter.

Remember, try to answer every question.

1. Developed by Alfred Binet, which of the following was originally designed to identify students with special learning needs?

    (A) Intelligence Quotient Test
    (B) Scholastic Assessment Test
    (C) Individual Education Program Test
    (D) Metropolitan Achievement Test
    (E) California Achievement Test

2. Magnet schools, which provide special curricula and/or pedagogical strategies, have been widely used in urban districts to

    (A) train children for specialized professions
    (B) improve educational efficiency
    (C) aid in development of an intellectual elite
    (D) desegregate the schools
    (E) attend to the special requirements of the urban workplace

3. A teacher receives an evaluation that she believes was poorly done because of the evaluator's lack of knowledge of the teacher's subject area. Which of the following is the best way for the teacher to voice her feeling that someone more qualified in the field should conduct another evaluation?

    (A) The teacher should write a letter to the superintendent of schools of her district demanding a new evaluation.
    (B) The teacher should discuss the evaluation with the evaluator, offering a counter-explanation of the poorly evaluated actions.
    (C) Confront the evaluator and let him know that the evaluation was unacceptable.
    (D) Speak to the curriculum specialist to determine which course of action should be followed.
    (E) Bring up the poor evaluation at a staff meeting in hopes that others have received poor evaluations, too.

4. Which of the following constitutes acceptable school prayer?

    (A) Private school prayer
    (B) Private student prayer
    (C) Whole-class prayer
    (D) Bible reading
    (E) A and B only

GO ON TO THE NEXT PAGE.

5. Mrs. White, a teacher of Advanced Placement English, wishes to improve her students' expository writing skills. Which of the following test types would best serve Mrs. White's purpose?

   (A) Essay
   (B) Fill-in-the-blank
   (C) Short-answer
   (D) Multiple-choice
   (E) Cloze test

6. Which is an example of de facto school segregation?

   (A) Segregation that occurs in schools as a result of ability grouping
   (B) Voluntary separation of students based on race within schools
   (C) State-mandated separation of students based on race
   (D) Separation of students based on race that occurs as the result of housing patterns
   (E) Separation of students based upon parental wishes

7. Which of the following is not a learning disability according to the Individuals with Disabilities Education Act (IDEA)?

   (A) Mental retardation
   (B) Speech or language impairment
   (C) Autism
   (D) Motor disability
   (E) Traumatic brain impairment

8. All of the following are reasons for employing cooperative learning strategies EXCEPT:

   (A) allows students to work in groups
   (B) encourages social interaction among students
   (C) fosters peer tutoring
   (D) makes work easier for students
   (E) improves students' peer-editing skills

9. Which of the following private school services can be secured with public funds?

   I.   Teaching personnel for special needs programs
   II. Religious instructional materials, e.g., scriptures
   III. Transportation for students who live more than two miles from the school

   (A) I only
   (B) II only
   (C) III only
   (D) I and II only
   (E) II and III only

10. Which of the following could be considered a revisionist historian?

   (A) Diane Ravitch
   (B) Howard Gardner
   (C) Colin Greer
   (D) Horace Mann
   (E) John Dewey

11. Title IX of the Education Amendments of 1972 says that the federal government will not support any institution that discriminates on the basis of gender. Which of the following would be <u>acceptable</u>, according to Title IX?

   (A) Separating boys and girls math classes to encourage girls' success in math
   (B) A religiously affiliated school separating boys and girls for an activity consistent with a particular tenent
   (C) Having only boys' varsity sports, but girls' junior varsity
   (D) Expecting boys and girls to perform the same physical education tasks
   (E) Forbidding boys to participate in the race for homecoming royalty

GO ON TO THE NEXT PAGE.

12. Mr. Johnson, a high-school social studies teacher, is trying to encourage more analytical thinking among his students. Which of the following questions would require the most analytical thinking skills and encourage them to adopt the broadest view of the topic?

    (A) What were some events that led to the perceived necessity of the Civil Rights Act of 1965?
    (B) Do you need civil rights? Why?
    (C) What was the Civil Rights Act of 1965?
    (D) Why was the Civil Rights Act of 1965 historically significant?
    (E) How did the signing of the Civil Rights Act of 1965 change the lives of citizens?

13. In December, Ms. Barbour, a third-grade teacher, wishes to teach a unit on winter holidays. Part of the unit discusses Christmas and Hanukkah. What should Ms. Barbour do before she begins her holiday unit?

    A) Speak to the principal about school policy regarding the discussion of matters involving religion
    B) Speak to students about their religious beliefs and preferences
    C) Nothing; the community is fairly inactive and will not object to a unit on holidays
    D) Consult the parents about how they would like the material to be presented
    E) Omit the unit, as any mention of Christmas or Hanukkah violates the separation of Church and State

14. Before beginning her grammar unit, Ms. Marshall gives her students a diagnostic grammar test to identify students' weaknesses. Such testing is characterized as

    (A) norm-referenced
    (B) haphazard
    (C) criterion-referenced
    (D) cloze testing
    (E) mind gaming

15. Horace Mann, an advocate of the common schools, suggested that they were necessary to

    (A) determine which citizens would be leaders
    (B) ensure that all citizens could master university-level material
    (C) encourage economic independence
    (D) provide insurance against societal ills
    (E) provide a vehicle by which citizens could maintain their ethnic heritage

16. *A Nation At Risk: Imperative for Educational Change* (1983) offered proposals meant to

    (A) improve race relations in the schools
    (B) create learning environments that encourage teacher decision-making
    (C) improve educational quality
    (D) embrace the tenets of multicultural education
    (E) raise the living standards of poor children

17. Which of the following is an important consideration when disciplining a student with disabilities?

    (A) The sympathy administrators have for students with disabilities
    (B) The degree to which their infraction may be related to their disability
    (C) The fact that students with disabilities are rarely discipline problems
    (D) The need exhibited by all students, regardless of disability, for occasional discipline
    (E) The degree to which the student understands the nature of the school rules

GO ON TO THE NEXT PAGE.

18. The *Pickering* (1968) case is important to aspiring teachers because

    (A) the case established the right of teachers to speak out on matters of public importance without being dismissed from their jobs for such speech
    (B) the case recommended due process for teacher dismissal
    (C) the case absolved teachers of responsibility to report suspected child abuse
    (D) the case determined the extent to which teachers are permitted to participate in hate-group activity
    (E) the case established the right of teachers to "come out of the closet" without being dismissed from their positions

19. A high-school English teacher who requires her students to memorize and recite Shakespeare's sonnets can explain her pedagogical decision based on which of the following theories?

    (A) Presentation and oratory skills are an important aspect of the formal communications process.
    (B) Shakespeare is best presented in dramatic form.
    (C) Shakespeare is the best author in English literature.
    (D) All secondary students are required to study Elizabethan Literature.
    (E) To memorize and recite a sonnet helps in comprehending the poet's ideas.

20. How did the adoption of the G.I. Bill of Rights change higher education in America?

    (A) G.I.'s were more dedicated students.
    (B) G.I.'s were more likely to have weapons on campus.
    (C) G.I.'s were usually older.
    (D) G.I.'s were more patriotic.
    (E) G.I.'s lowered academic standards.

21. One of the most common justifications for block scheduling at the high-school level is

    (A) that research proves that teachers need more structure in order to get to know their students
    (B) that students perform worse on standardized tests with such scheduling
    (C) that such scheduling allows for more instructional time
    (D) that studies show that students spend less time in the hallway
    (E) that students who spend more time in each class enjoy their classes more

22. A fourth-grade teacher wishes to improve the reading level of those students who have been labeled "slow learners." Which of the following is a method of boosting students' reading levels and improving self-esteem?

    (A) Having "slow" students tutored by older students
    (B) Having "slow" students tutor younger students
    (C) Having "slow" students tutored by their parents
    (D) Sending "slow" students to remedial classes
    (E) Giving "slow" students cloze passages

23. Site-based management is characterized by

    (A) bottom-up decision making
    (B) greater central office input
    (C) teachers and administrators both having input into how the school is run
    (D) less teacher autonomy
    (E) a more bureaucratic structure

GO ON TO THE NEXT PAGE.

24. Ability grouping (tracking) is frequently criticized for

   (A) being too rigorous a program of study at the lowest levels
   (B) including too many students in the upper levels
   (C) encouraging movement between levels
   (D) disregarding the intellectual ability of gifted students
   (E) segregating students based upon socio-economic status

25. Who is best known for promoting de-schooling?

   (A) Milton Friedman
   (B) Horace Mann
   (C) Ivan Illich
   (D) Ronald Reagan
   (E) Malcolm X

26. Which of the following best describes the Freedman's Education movement?

   (A) A period of education innovation promoted by Walter Freedman
   (B) The schooling of the former slaves during Reconstruction
   (C) A system of Jewish immigrant education in New York City around the turn of the century
   (D) A plan characterized by open floor plans for elementary-schoolers
   (E) The formal categorization of rehabilitative education provided for convicts

27. A teacher objects to reciting the Pledge of Allegiance on the basis of her religious beliefs. Which is the most appropriate course of action for the teacher to take?

   A) The teacher should teach in a private school
   B) The teacher should stand before the flag and not recite the pledge
   C) The teacher should facilitate a situation where a student leads the pledge with other interested students
   D) The teacher should suggest to the principal that the pledge not be a part of the morning activity
   E) The teacher should explain her objections to the students and refrain from reciting the pledge

GO ON TO THE NEXT PAGE.

Question 28 refers to the passage below.

Listening tests are very important to student assessment from the standpoint of oral communication. Students need to understand talks and lectures. Also, many students must use TV programs, movies, and radio as supplemental sources of information in their learning processes. These can often be very different from what students are accustomed to in their native cultures. Finally, all students need to understand transactions: asking and receiving directions, polite exchange, and other vital face-to-face meetings where listening acuity is particularly important.

28. This passage would be applicable to which of the following teaching disciplines?

(A) Mathematics education
(B) Special education
(C) Language education
(D) Educational leadership
(E) Speech pathology

Questions 29-30 are based on the following passage.

Student self-assessment is a tool that is very effective in the science classroom. One of the real benefits of using performance-assessment tasks is the opportunity that it gives students to take part in the assessment process. When assessment is viewed as an integral part of the instructional process, focus shifts from "giving tests" to helping students understand the goals of the learning experience and the criteria for success.

29. According to the passage above, which of the following BEST summarizes the use of self-assessment in the science classroom?

(A) Students feel more connected to their learning, from planning to grading lessons.
(B) Students build more self-esteem, making them want to participate in classroom activities.
(C) Students understand the difficulties teachers have in planning effective testing strategies.
(D) Students can interact verbally during the discussion section of the lesson
(E) Teachers have an easier time administering tests to students.

30. This passage supplies information that answers which of the following questions?

(A) What are the different kinds of assessment tools available to the science teacher?
(B) What is meant by "self-actualized learning development"?
(C) How can teachers integrate self assessment techniques across curriculums?
(D) What are alternative forms of self-assessment used in middle schools today?
(E) None of the above.

GO ON TO THE NEXT PAGE.

31. An eighth-grade Language Arts teacher wishes to assign a nineteenth-century novel that uses racial epithets that are objectionable to African Americans, the students whom he teaches. Any of the following approaches may be appropriate to prepare students to comprehend the social climate in which the novel was written EXCEPT

    (A) a brief explanation of the social climate of the times, stressing that what was acceptable behavior then may be unacceptable now
    (B) discuss with students the likelihood of hearing such language
    (C) a discussion of how words can hurt
    (D) introducing the novel with a passage that uses the epithet and generating a discussion about how and why the author chose that particular language
    (E) having students write a story using language that is not commonly used in school but would be understood by most people of their generation

32. The Progressive Education movement is responsible for all of the following educational reform ideas EXCEPT

    (A) alternative schools
    (B) student-centered instruction
    (C) learning by doing
    (D) curriculum reform
    (E) collaborative endeavors

33. Howard Gardner, an educational psychologist, has suggested that the traditional Intelligence Quotient Test is faulty because it does not account for many factors that comprise "intelligence." Gardner suggests at least seven broad categories of intelligence. Which one of the following is a category which he would NOT recognize?

    (A) Logical-mathematical
    (B) Spatial
    (C) Bodily-kinesthetic
    (D) Age-appropriate maturity
    (E) Musical

GO ON TO THE NEXT PAGE.

34. Each of the following is an example of an "objective test" item EXCEPT

   (A) "Write the chemical symbol for copper."
   (B) "Who is the poet who wrote 'A Dream Deferred'?"
   (C) "Explain the philosophy and rationale behind the New Deal."
   (D) "True or False: Pennsylvania was the first state in the union."
   (E) "'Four score and seven years ago...' begins what famous speech?"

35. Inclusion of special education students in "regular" classes is promoted for all of the following reasons EXCEPT

   (A) to create a diverse learning environment
   (B) to promote tolerance for those with disabilities among the non-disabled
   (C) to insure that all students learn the warning signs of various disabilities
   (D) to provide the "least restrictive environment" for students with handicaps
   (E) to improve the social skills of handicapped students

S T O P

THIS IS THE END OF THIS SECTION.
IF YOU FINISH BEFORE TIME IS CALLED, YOU MAY CHECK YOUR WORK ON THIS SECTION ONLY.
DO NOT WORK ON ANY OTHER SECTION IN THE TEST.

SECTION 2

Time–30 minutes

Directions: Each of the questions or incomplete statements below is followed by five suggested answers or completions. Select the one that is best in each case and then fill in the corresponding lettered space on the answer sheet with a heavy, dark mark so that you cannot see the letter.

Remember, try to answer every question.

1. Comprehensive school services include all but which of the following?

    (A) Parental and community involvement
    (B) Coordination of federal, state, local, and private resources
    (C) Day-care for children of school-aged teenagers
    (D) Research-based methods
    (E) Consistent evaluation strategies

2. Jonathan Kozol criticizes public schooling because of his belief that schools

    (A) fail in their service of poor and minority children
    (B) encourage competition among students
    (C) are poorly built
    (D) focus too much attention on academics and not enough on social development
    (E) are structured in such a way that teachers are left powerless

3. One of the reasons for great disparities in funding of school districts within a state is that

    (A) the best schools get the most money
    (B) federal programs aid poor school districts more than wealthy ones
    (C) property taxes fund local school districts
    (D) some school districts conduct huge fund-raising projects
    (E) students are charged tuition to attend schools outside of their districts

4. Those opposed to voucher plans for schooling would agree with which of the following statements?

    (A) School decisions are better left to those who have the most expertise: central office personnel.
    (B) Competition encourages higher quality.
    (C) The political arena is the proper regulator of school policy.
    (D) Funding should be attached to institutions, not individuals
    (E) Religion should be taught in public schools.

5. A researcher follows the academic achievement of Head Start students throughout their primary and secondary schooling. Such a study can be best characterized as

    (A) economic/ethnographic
    (B) historical
    (C) quantitative
    (D) latitudinal
    (E) longitudinal

6. One of the most important elements of maintaining effective classroom discipline is

    (A) strictness
    (B) consistency
    (C) inflexibility
    (D) knowing who is "good" and who is "bad"
    (E) formality

GO ON TO THE NEXT PAGE.

7. An elementary-school teacher goes over answers to questions on an exam after the exam has been taken, graded, and handed back to students. She then allows students to resubmit corrected "wrong" answers to improve their grades. This teacher is practicing which teaching method?

(A) Holistic assessment
(B) Editing
(C) Webbing
(D) Review and revision
(E) None of the above

8. Mr. Jones, a fourth-grade teacher, is informed by one of his students that Jack (a disruptive student in Mr. Jones's class) has cigarettes in his desk. Possession of tobacco on school grounds is against school policy. Mr. Jones goes into Jack's desk and finds not only cigarettes but also a knife. Mr. Jones reports this discovery to the school principal. Which of the following will likely happen as the result of Mr. Jones' actions?

(A) Jack will sue Mr. Jones for invasion of privacy.
(B) Jack will be questioned but not disciplined because Mr. Jones was not authorized to search Jack's desk.
(C) Jack will be suspended from school for possession of a weapon
(D) Jack will be forced to give his knife and cigarettes to Mr. Jones
(E) None of the above.

9. The 1954 case *Brown v. the Board of Education of Topeka, KS,*

(A) insured equal educational funding for all students
(B) insured the desegregation of all white schools
(C) compelled school districts to bus students
(D) compelled school districts to decentralize authority
(E) is currently being re-examined by the Supreme Court

10. Rolanda, an eighth-grade student, comes into class wearing her traditional ethnic garb. Her dress is the topic of conversation and derogatory comments among some of the students in the class. What is the most appropriate way to handle Rolanda's ethnic expression?

(A) Ask Rolanda to tone down her dress, as it is disruptive to the class.
(B) Tell Rolanda that such dress is inappropriate in America.
(C) Incorporate student comments into a lesson encouraging positive reflection
(D) Point out another student's outfit and ask the class to critique it.
(E) Talk to Rolanda's counselor about a probable identity crisis.

11. The school newspaper prints a story that accuses a teacher of grade inflation. What practical recourse does the teacher have?

(A) Suing the system for libel
(B) Assigning a failing grade to the student-editor
(C) Holding a conference with the student-editor and faculty moderator
(D) Writing an inflammatory letter to the school newspaper calling the author of the article a liar
(E) Harassing the moderator of the newspaper

GO ON TO THE NEXT PAGE.

12. Mindy, a student who is known for her attention-seeking behavior, relays to Mr. Ramsey (her tenth-grade physical education teacher), that she often has thoughts of suicide. What would be the most appropriate action for Mr. Ramsey to take?

    (A) He should ignore it, because Mindy is always seeking attention.
    (B) He should call a suicide hotline and ask for advice.
    (C) He should get in touch with Mindy's guidance counselor.
    (D) He should call Mindy's parents and tell them to keep a watch out.
    (E) He should alert all of Mindy's teachers.

13. According to Madeline Hunter, which of the following is needed in order for students to prepare for homework assignments?

    (A) Verbal corroboration from the teacher about which assignment to complete
    (B) Guided practice during class time that replicates the work assigned
    (C) Contact with guidance counselors regarding the efficacy of homework
    (D) A principal's interaction with students when homework is not completed
    (E) Numeric grades for every third assignment given

14. Norm-referenced test data could be deemed reliable in which one of the following situations?

    (A) When every fifth-grader in the state has taken the exam
    (B) When random samples of fifth-graders have been used in multiple pilot studies and results have been shown to be statistically the same
    (C) When studies have used multiple-regression techniques to interpret data
    (D) When the data has been interpreted by a professional
    (E) When the interpreter has an opportunity to review the writing samples of more than one sample population

15. Which type of questioning scheme would be best suited for assessing students' knowledge of science processes?

    (A) Cloze questions
    (B) Open-ended questions
    (C) Multiple-choice questions
    (D) Rote memorization
    (E) Matching questions

16. Which is a valid factor that influences a second-language learner's acquisition progress?

    I. The student's sex
    II. The student's native language
    III. The student's level of education in his or her native language

    (A) I only
    (B) II only
    (C) I and II only
    (D) II and III only
    (E) I, II, and III

17. How would a seventh-grade teacher of literature best modify her instructional strategy to include increasing comprehension for the auditory learner?

    (A) Have the students read the story out loud
    (B) Have a cassette tape available for students to record the teacher reading the story
    (C) Have students write an essay on the plot development of the story, investigating the use of religious motifs
    (D) Have students build a model of the home where the story takes place, to show its setting
    (E) Have students take a conversation between two characters in the story and, using role-play, verbally devise other plausible scenarios that explore options in the plot

GO ON TO THE NEXT PAGE.

18. When teaching students paragraph writing, it is understood that the topic sentence must

    (A) always be the first sentence in the paragraph
    (B) be highlighted in bold letters
    (C) contain any citations that relate to the subject of the essay
    (D) precede supporting examples through-out the paragraph that defend or illustrate the point made
    (E) be phrased rhetorically

19. A sixth-grade student's family converts to Islam. Subsequently, the girl's dress changes to reflect her family's beliefs. Her parents assert that she cannot undress in front of her female classmates, nor wear shorts for physical education, because they feel that such actions violate Islamic teachings. What is an acceptable way of having the student fulfill the state's physical education requirement?

    (A) There is no way that the student can fulfill the requirement without un-dressing and wearing the shorts and tennis shoes that everyone else wears.
    (B) Inform the principal of the problem, and allow him/her to handle it.
    (C) Inform the principal and/or counselor of the situation, then consult the parents, to mediate a solution that all three parties can agree upon.
    (D) Verify that what the parents say about their beliefs is true.
    (E) Call an Islamic clergyman and ask for advice.

20. A new teacher seems to have trouble with classroom management. His students do not respect him and are disruptive during his class periods. The same students do not show behavioral problems with another new teacher, who teaches across the hall. Which of the following is the best interpretation of the situation?

    (A) The students are ill-behaved and are in need of punishment.
    (B) The first teacher has not devoted suffi-cient time to explaining the rules of classroom behavior.
    (C) The first teacher should integrate a system of rewards and consequences into a daily academic structure
    (D) The students do not know the new teacher's rules of classroom behavior.
    (E) The students may have psychological problems related to their behavior and should be seen by the guidance counselor.

21. Which of the following is an example of learning with the aid of a mnemonic device?

    (A) A student devises a system for remem-bering the steps of a geometry theo-rem that uses the first letters of the alphabet for each axiom or corollary.
    (B) A student reads a list of terms, but not their meanings, between 4 and 6 PM every day, so that she can memorize them for a test.
    (C) A student works with a tutor for three weeks, practicing exercises and dialogues for a Spanish test.
    (D) A student crams for a history oral exam the night before the test.
    (E) A student uses her "photographic" memory, which enables her to recall most of what she reads.

GO ON TO THE NEXT PAGE.

22. A teacher notices that her ninth-grade student is intellectually bright, but socially immature. Instead of having conversations and establishing relationships with members of the opposite sex, he is sarcastic and verbally abusive toward them, frequently disrupting lessons. What should the teacher do to assist the student in his social development and to eliminate the disruptions in her class?

(A) Consult the student's guidance counselor about the boy's misogynistic tendencies.

(B) Consult the department's assistant principal about the student and ask her to set up an interview with the student.

(C) Speak with the student, gaining his trust, and try to counsel him about speaking to girls.

(D) Inform the student that his behavior during class is unacceptable, and talk to his parents.

(E) Discipline the student when he acts inappropriately in class, and do not address his problems with the opposite sex.

23. According to current research, which of the following has the strongest relationship to student achievement?

(A) Teacher training
(B) Teacher experience
(C) The textbook publisher
(D) Per capita income of the student's community
(E) Student/teacher ratios

24. Students whose parents speak a language other than English at home

(A) should try to take science and history classes in their language one

(B) must show that they are American citizens before they can be enrolled in school

(C) must receive benefits and services from the federal government to assist them in learning English

(D) should undergo a Home Language Survey to ascertain whether the student is in need of language services

(E) are not entitled to any federal benefits or protections based on linguistic orientation

25. Which of the following is an example of "mainstreaming"?

(A) A student enters a new class from another school district.

(B) A student studies subjects relating to the environment and ecological protection.

(C) A minority student is integrated in a majority classroom.

(D) A hearing-impaired student takes classes with non-hearing-impaired students.

(E) A developmentally-challenged student receives services in a school designed for students like him, in order to prepare him for the outside world.

GO ON TO THE NEXT PAGE.

26. Shy or withdrawn students are more likely to participate in a lesson if
    I. they are told about it the day before
    II. they are asked to analyze a reading selection for their homework
    III. they are asked to present a part of the lesson in front of the class
    IV. they are verbally praised in class by their peers
    V. they are encouraged to take small risks in front of the class, increasing their involvement as time progresses

    (A) I only
    (B) I and II only
    (C) III and IV only
    (D) III, IV, and V only
    (E) IV and V only

27. Madeline Hunter's concept of a "warm-up" exercise is BEST exemplified by which of the following ?

    (A) The teacher enters the class and starts to write questions on the board related to the previous day's lesson for review before she moves on to a new lesson.
    (B) The teacher spends time chatting with the class about the school team's recent basketball game before introducing the new lesson.
    (C) The teacher asks if there are any questions about last night's homework.
    (D) The teacher passes out in-class work from two days earlier.
    (E) The teacher moves into the lesson gradually, spending social and short on-task time with students for about 10 minutes before moving into the lesson for the day.

28. "Drug-free zone" is a term that describes
    I. an area where no one can use drugs in the community
    II. a prescribed area in a community, that citizens work together to rid of the sales, distribution, and use of drugs
    III. a prescribed area around a school where the fines for drug-related infractions are stiffer than they are in the general community

    (A) I only
    (B) II only
    (C) III only
    (D) I and II only
    (E) II and III only

GO ON TO THE NEXT PAGE.

Questions 29-30 are based on the following passage.

It is ironic that the devices and systems of technology, which hold the promise of freeing man to become more human, also portend the danger of diminishing our humanity. In education, we have made the error of seeking to use the devices and systems of technology to restrict our notion of human behavior. We have become less tolerant of ambiguity, digression, divergence, and expression of feeling—all characteristically human qualities.

29. This passage is essentially a discussion of

(A) technological intrusions in education today
(B) concerns about the use of computers in the classroom
(C) the devices and systems of educational technology currently in use
(D) the benefits of a technological curriculum
(E) the fears aroused by advances in technology

30. According to the author, what are the results of the use of technology in education?

(A) Restrictions on free expression in young people
(B) Promises of advances in education that technology cannot deliver
(C) The removal of all traces of diversity in thought, feeling, and behavior
(D) The creation of a learning environment too complex for our schoolchildren
(E) The diminution of the need for humans in the educational system

31. All of the following characterize state legislation regarding handicapped children EXCEPT

(A) no handicapped child will be excluded from services
(B) appropriations will be earmarked for special education
(C) records regarding handicapped children are public
(D) sanctions will be designated for local education authorities that do not comply with state law
(E) procedural due process will be followed for determining placement of students in special education

32. Critics of multicultural education cite all of the following as problems inherent in multiculturalism EXCEPT

(A) multiculturalism is ethnically divisive
(B) multicultural education "waters down" the curriculum
(C) students do not have a common schooling experience with multicultural education
(D) multicultural education fosters respect for America's diverse ethnic heritage
(E) multicultural education does not embrace the precepts of Western Civilization

33. Ms. Smith is attempting to model good learning behavior for her twelfth-grade students. She should do all of the following EXCEPT

(A) encourage feedback on the effectiveness of lessons presented
(B) stress the reciprocal nature of the classroom learning experience
(C) reprimand students when they are critical of her pedagogical methods
(D) praise students for pointing out any teacher error
(E) make mention of her learning experiences outside the classroom

GO ON TO THE NEXT PAGE.

34. Kohlberg's principles of moral development include all of the following EXCEPT

   (A) progression proceeds through one stage at a time
   (B) regression is theoretically impossible
   (C) moral thinking may be internally inconsistent
   (D) most adults reach the third level of moral thinking
   (E) individuals can skip over certain developmental stages

35. A Life Science teacher of middle school students could pose all of the following questions to assess students' problem solving skills EXCEPT

   (A) "Can you explain the question in your own words?"
   (B) "What are the steps you would use to isolate the components of this question?"
   (C) "How do you operationally define this question?"
   (D) "Is this the right answer to this question?"
   (E) "Explain the method you used to find the answer to this question."

S T O P

THIS IS THE END OF THIS SECTION.
IF YOU FINISH BEFORE TIME IS CALLED, YOU MAY CHECK YOUR WORK ON THIS SECTION ONLY.
DO NOT WORK ON ANY OTHER SECTION IN THE TEST.

SECTION 3

Time–30 minutes

Directions: Each of the questions or incomplete statements below is followed by five suggested answers or completions. Select the one that is best in each case and then fill in the corresponding lettered space on the answer sheet with a heavy, dark mark so that you cannot see the letter.

Remember, try to answer every question.

1. Out of a class of 25 students, ten fail to master the concepts of a lesson presented by the teacher as part of a thematic unit. In response, the teacher should

  (A) ask the ten students why they didn't understand the concepts, and re-teach them; at the same time, give the fifteen students who do understand the concepts more advanced work

  (B) move on to the next set of concepts, but at a slower pace

  (C) ask the students to explain what they understand up to the point where they begin to become confused

  (D) stop the unit and allow the slower students to catch up before the entire class moves on

  (E) use a multifaceted strategy employing peer teaching, cooperative learning strategies, and supplemental approaches and materials to help the ten master the concepts, and keep the entire class moving ahead.

2. Due to rapid school growth, students and teachers are asked to use trailers adjacent to the school building for classrooms. When students object to having to walk outside to attend classes, the teacher can help facilitate a resolution to the objection by saying which of the following?

  (A) "You students should be happy that you even have a classroom at all!"

  (B) "You have a point; I don't like walking outside to go to my classroom either. Why don't we all go speak to the principal?"

  (C) "This decision was not made here at school. Ask your parents to call the School Board."

  (D) "It's not my fault, so I don't want to hear it. Take out last night's homework."

  (E) "Can we think of some ways that we might be able to balance the inconvenience with the fact that we have a new space dedicated to our needs alone?"

GO ON TO THE NEXT PAGE.

3. When explaining the concept of oral history to a seventh-grade social studies class, the BEST instructional strategy would be to

(A) have an English professor from a local university explain the concept of oral tradition to the students
(B) have the students look up "oral tradition" in the library
(C) have students listen to tapes of oral histories from the Smithsonian
(D) have the students learn some of their own oral histories from their families, and have them recount them to their classmates
(E) have the students read *The Story of Miss Jane Pittman* aloud in class

4. When preparing a cloze test to assess the comprehension of a historical narrative, the teacher should take which of the following steps?

 I.   Select an appropriate passage
 II. Decide on the number of words to take out
 III. Write instructions and prepare an example

(A) I only
(B) I and II only
(C) I and III only
(D) I, II, and III only
(E) II and III only

5. Which of the following is the best assessment method for testing in biology?

(A) Norm-referenced tests
(B) Oral interview
(C) Portfolio
(D) Mixed multiple-choice and short answer tests
(E) Limited-response cloze tests

6. The term "intelligence" is commonly regarded as

(A) an absolute value within a society or group of citizens in a country
(B) a term denoting the level of formal education received during one's lifetime
(C) interchangeable with the term "aptitude"
(D) a multifaceted term that includes verbal ability, cognitive functions, and certain subject-specific reasoning skills
(E) a complex series of measurements based on population means, describing functions, academic achievement, and aptitudes

7. Norm-referenced tests are BEST designed to rate students in which of the following ways?

(A) By comparing students to their classmates, using a general body of knowledge
(B) By comparing students to certain standards, regardless of how other students fare on the exam
(C) By rating students on overall mastery of the concepts presented
(D) By giving students a test that combines various sub-skills that are designed to mimic real life
(E) By measuring students' progress from one point in time to another

GO ON TO THE NEXT PAGE.

8. What is the primary purpose of vocabulary tests?

(A) To measure how many new words students have learned in the unit

(B) To measure the comprehension and production of words used in speaking or writing

(C) To measure vocabulary mastery in a second-language context

(D) To provide the teacher with an effective tool for measuring the effectiveness of homework

(E) To have students memorize a primary list of useful words that they will need in the future

9. Which one of the following trends could be categorized under the general title of "School Reform"?

(A) After five years of satisfactory evaluations, teachers are issued a "lifetime certification."

(B) School districts consult teachers on the choice of textbooks for future use.

(C) Alternative certification training is provided to teachers in content areas where eligible candidates are few.

(D) Parental empowerment is strengthened through the use of school choice vouchers.

(E) Key decisions for a particular school are placed in the hands of principals, parents, and teachers.

10. The theory of "cultural literacy" is best expressed by which of the following statements?

I. Children should be aware of their cultural heritage.

II. Children should be knowledgeable about the varying cultures that comprise American society.

III. Children should have a general frame of reference including names, dates, and achievements that symbolize Western cultural achievement.

(A) I only
(B) II only
(C) III only
(D) I and II only
(E) I, II and III

11. Bloom's Taxonomy was a classification system that sought to

(A) organize learning into units understandable to students

(B) classify the levels of thinking behaviors that are important in the learning process

(C) separate learning objectives into affective domains

(D) identify the nine levels of knowledge

(E) None of the above.

12. Which of the following would be the best application of a norm-referenced instrument?

(A) A sixth-grade literature exam for 25 children

(B) An exam used to determine Spanish literacy at the intermediate language level

(C) A quiz in calculus for a university freshman class of 250 students

(D) A test to measure reading levels of fourth graders in New Mexico

(E) None of the above

GO ON TO THE NEXT PAGE.

13. According to theories of multicultural education, the process of "acculturation" takes place when

(A) students are able to speak English fluently

(B) parents are able to understand the school district's educational goals

(C) students are able to choose between their former and present cultures

(D) students choose which cultural values to retain from their past and which to adopt from their present situation

(E) students obtain American citizenship

14. An individualized learning program (ILP) is required for students who

(A) have completed a diagnostic process for exceptional children

(B) exhibit a pattern of behavioral problems in class

(C) are withdrawn from school for medical reasons

(D) have shown a lack of progress in the past marking session

(E) have entered the school in mid-session

15. Which of the following is a valid reason for consulting the school psychologist?

(A) A child's grades are falling, yet the level of effort remains the same.

(B) A child has recurring bouts of violence within a period of a few days.

(C) A child complains of being abused at home by a parent.

(D) A child seems physically immature for his age, and his classmates tease him.

(E) All of the above.

16. Bilingualism is defined as

(A) the ability to read two languages

(B) the ability to communicate in any form in two languages

(C) the need to communicate important ideas in the more proficient language

(D) the knowledge of more than one language

(E) the ability to read, write, speak, and listen in two languages

17. Under the Privacy Act of 1974, which of the following is permissible?

(A) A teacher can remove a bundle from a student's pocket after the student has stated that the bundle contains an illegal drug.

(B) A principal can search a student's locker for drugs without a warrant.

(C) A teacher may call a student's parent to inquire why the student is absent from school.

(D) A student may view his or her own confidential records upon request.

(E) A counselor may discuss a student's parents with other teachers over lunch.

18. A school counselor wishes to conduct a study of all the students in her school. After notifying parents and speaking to students about the study, the counselor should

(A) begin comparing students based on non-equivalent groups

(B) inform teachers about what conclusions she hopes to draw from the study

(C) gather feedback from colleagues and administrators about the study

(D) withhold details of her preparation from other counselors

(E) publicly announce the names of those students who refuse to participate in the study

GO ON TO THE NEXT PAGE.

19. For homework, students are asked to write stories based on their personal experiences. One student's story closely resembles one written over fifty years ago by a well-known author. The teacher notices the similarity and holds a conference with the student to find out if the story is authentic. Which of the following statements is appropriate when approaching the student?

   (A) "I'm not sure this is an example of your work. Are you familiar with the rules on plagiarism?"
   (B) "This story is clearly too well written to be your work."
   (C) "What makes you think that you can deceive a teacher and get away with it?"
   (D) "Even the best authors copy other authors' work, so don't hesitate to do it again."
   (E) "Your story was quite well written. See if you can write a few more paragraphs in class for me, so that I will know a little more about you."

20. Which of the following is an appropriate diagnosis for a teacher to make of a student whose handwriting is poor, whose behavior is disruptive, and who shows little ability to follow instructions?

   (A) The student may be frustrated by challenging new assignments.
   (B) The student has dyslexia.
   (C) The student has Attention Deficit Hyperactivity Disorder (ADHD).
   (D) The student suffers from domestic abuse.
   (E) The student resents and dislikes authority figures.

21. Psychological testing is most commonly recommended for its ability to

   (A) encourage client dependency on the counselor
   (B) detect and recognize psychological differences among ethnic groups
   (C) advance the placement of students into suitable educational and career situations
   (D) influence fellow students' understanding of a student's behavior
   (E) reliably address the difficulties that students have in the classroom and at home

22. A fifth-grade geography teacher needs to present a lesson on Mediterranean Europe. Which of the following would be included in the lesson?

   (A) An analysis of the geological history of the Pyrenees Mountains
   (B) A discussion of recent terrorist activity in the Middle East
   (C) A discussion of the region's cultural and religious traditions
   (D) An explanation of Spain's relationship with Nazi Germany during World War II
   (E) An in-class project exploring the physical differences between Northern European and Mediterranean peoples

GO ON TO THE NEXT PAGE.

23. A student who displays a high degree of anxiety before a mathematics test is most likely

    (A) suffering from innumeracy (the inability to understand arithmetic)
    (B) exhibiting signs of domestic abuse
    (C) experiencing test-taking anxiety
    (D) suffering from dyslexia
    (E) seeking attention from teachers and peers

24. Which of the following are good reasons for teaching dictionary usage?

    I. Exploring word origins
    II. Verifying correct spelling
    III. Finding antonyms to words

    (A) I only
    (B) II only
    (C) I and II only
    (D) I and III only
    (E) I, II, and III

25. Which of the following represents the best method of informing students about their progress in class?

    (A) "Your work is generally good, except for your performance in math, science, social studies, and language arts."
    (B) "Your work is so bad that I cannot explain it to you at all."
    (C) "Although you show little progress so far, I think that it's best if we wait until the end of the term to discuss it."
    (D) "This week, let's talk about your trouble spelling words with double letters and the progress you've made adding fractions."
    (E) "Despite the difficulty that you're having in geography, I think we should forget about it and talk about your great work in math class."

Questions 26-28 are based on the following passage.

The difficulties teachers face when working with language minority students are very real, and they go far beyond the day-to-day problems inherent in trying to teach students who aren't proficient in English. In essence, a teacher's job is made more demanding by non-pedagogical issues and conflicting goals related to implementing bilingual education. As members of American society and as torchbearers for American culture, teachers may feel compelled to adopt the view that language minority students should be mainstreamed as quickly as possible. The community may also occasionally resent the funding of bilingual programs when they perceive that these funds could go toward enhancing the traditional curriculum.

It seems clear, however, that more is involved in educating language minority students than providing them with drills and exercises related to English grammar or reclassifying them into English-only classes as quickly as possible. It may take years for language minority students to become literate in academic English. No one's interests are served if they are reclassified too early, for their ultimate personal failure is also a social, an institutional, and a professional one. The situation calls for a reevaluation of what successful instruction should be.

26. The passage addresses the needs of which population of students?

    (A) Those with language processing difficulties
    (B) Those who are culturally disadvantaged due to poor language usage
    (C) Those who are from a different ethnic background
    (D) Those who are handicapped
    (E) Those whose second language is English

GO ON TO THE NEXT PAGE.

27. The passage asserts that teachers may have which of the following concerns when teaching language minority students?

(A) Their students may be illiterate in English grammar and in the traditional curriculum.

(B) Their students may be forced to enter mainstreamed classes before they are ready.

(C) Their students may have more than the obvious number of instructional problems due to their minority status.

(D) Teachers may not want to teach language minority students.

(E) Teachers may want more money for teaching the traditional curriculum.

28. In the first paragraph, what is meant by "non-pedagogical issues" related to implementing bilingual education?

 I. The community may not want to spend money to educate non-native speakers of English.

 II. Students may have cultural adjustment issues related to the classroom environment.

 III. Some teachers may not have enough time and resources effectively to teach the students English and another language.

(A) I only

(B) II only

(C) III only

(D) I and II only

(E) II and III only

29. Paul, an eighth-grade student, writes an essay that begins, "When we was young an all, we all use to go out to my granddaddy farm down by root 29." Paul's writing exhibits which of the following?

 I. Usage common in Paul's environment

 II. Paul's unfamiliarity with the difference between formal and colloquial language

 III. Paul's need for instruction in spelling, grammar, and usage in the context of expository writing

(A) I only

(B) II only

(C) I and II only

(D) I and III only

(E) I, II, and III

30. Instructional planning is most effective when which of the following is taken into account?

(A) The individual facts students must learn

(B) The methods by which students learn

(C) An individual teacher's knowledge

(D) The tastes of parents and administrators

(E) Students' desire to learn

GO ON TO THE NEXT PAGE.

31. Which of the following statements is NOT true regarding the certification of professional teachers?

    (A) Full-time teachers are certified to teach in any of the fifty states and territories
    (B) Full-time teachers must possess at minimum a bachelor's degree in order to be issued a state certificate
    (C) Teachers must be trained in the state where they apply for certification
    (D) Generally, teachers must have no felony criminal record in order to be certified
    (E) Teachers must fulfill any professional requirements (professional competency or physical exams, practice teaching, etc.) as required by the state within the prescribed time limits before a permanent certificate can be issued.

32. Webbing (or Brainstorming) is a Whole Language technique that is LEAST likely to be effective in which of the following circumstances?

    (A) When students are asked to give responses on what they know about spiders
    (B) When students are asked to provide various mathematical values between 1.0 and 3.5
    (C) When students are shown the cover of a book with a picture of wild birds, and are asked to free-associate
    (D) When students are asked to calculate the hypoteneuse of an obtuse triangle
    (E) When students are asked to list some of the results of Jeffersonian Democracy

33. A teacher wishes to present a math lesson on budgeting (gaining control over income and spending). Which of the following is LEAST likely to be used as a model for this lesson?

    (A) The salary of Sally Jones, a mother of two children
    (B) The balance sheet for Ames Elementary School for the academic year 1994-1995
    (C) The ledger of Zack Graham, a city taxicab driver
    (D) A copy of the state legislative record
    (E) A receipt from Food Star grocery store

34. A class of third-graders from a city elementary school is to visit a rural area to see a farm. All of the following lessons would be appropriate to teach before the trip EXCEPT a lesson about

    (A) the types of men who become farmers
    (B) the machinery used on a modern farm, and how it differs from older tools
    (C) typical animals on a farm, and what they produce
    (D) how farmers bring goods to market
    (E) parts of the state where most farms are located

35. Which of the following is NOT currently a trend in education in the United States?

    (A) National certification of teachers, instead of only on the state level
    (B) Giving parents a choice to have their children attend either a public or private school at state expense
    (C) Attempts in some districts to reintroduce Christian prayer in public schools
    (D) The creation of public schools in which the curricula, instructional practices, and the hiring of teachers follow an Afro-centric orientation
    (E) State-mandated corporal punishment for student misbehavior

STOP

THIS IS THE END OF THIS SECTION.
IF YOU FINISH BEFORE TIME IS CALLED, YOU MAY CHECK YOUR WORK ON THIS SECTION ONLY.
DO NOT WORK ON ANY OTHER SECTION IN THE TEST.

NTE DIAGNOSTIC ANSWER KEY

Section 1 Social Studies	Section 2 Math	Section 3 Literature and Fine Arts	Section 4 Science	Section 1 Listening	Section 2 Reading
1. B	1. D		1. C	1. B	1. E
2. D	2. C	1. D	2. A	2. B	2. E
3. A	3. A	2. B	3. E	3. C	3. C
4. B	4. D	3. D	4. A	4. C	4. B
5. E	5. B	4. D	5. C	5. D	5. C
6. C	6. C	5. B	6. D	6. A	6. B
7. A	7. A	6. E	7. A	7. D	7. C
8. E	8. D	7. B	8. C	8. D	8. D
9. C	9. E	8. C	9. D	9. C	9. E
10. A	10. A	9. A	10. E	10. B	10. B
11. D	11. E	10. A	11. B	11. B	11. D
12. D	12. E	11. E	12. B	12. C	12. E
13. D	13. C	12. A	13. C	13. C	13. C
14. A	14. A	13. C	14. D	14. A	14. A
15. D	15. C	14. B	15. B	15. B	15. B
16. D	16. C	15. C	16. C	16. C	16. A
17. A	17. D	16. E	17. A	17. A	17. A
18. E	18. D	17. B	18. E	18. D	18. E
19. E	19. B	18. C	19. D	19. B	19. D
20. B	20. D	19. D	20. C	20. B	20. A
21. B	21. B	20. D	21. E	21. C	21. B
22. C	22. E	21. E	22. D	22. D	22. D
23. A	23. B	22. B	23. C	23. C	23. D
24. C	24. E	23. B	24. A	24. D	24. D
25. D	25. D	24. C	25. C	25. C	25. C
26. C		25. C	26. B	26. D	26. D
27. B		26. A	27. C	27. A	27. C
28. D		27. C	28. D	28. C	28. A
29. D		28. C	29. B	29. A	29. C
30. B		29. D	30. C	30. B	30. C
		30. E		31. C	
		31. D		32. C	
		32. C		33. A	
		33. A		34. D	
		34. D		35. B	
		35. C		36. C	
				37. A	
				38. C	
				39. A	
				40. D	

Section 3 Writing		Section 1		Section 2		Section 3	
1.	B	1.	A	1.	C	1.	E
2.	B	2.	D	2.	A	2.	E
3.	C	3.	B	3.	C	3.	E
4.	E	4.	E	4.	D	4.	E
5.	B	5.	A	5.	A	5.	D
6.	C	6.	A	6.	B	6.	D
7.	D	7.	D	7.	D	7.	A
8.	D	8.	D	8.	C	8.	B
9.	E	9.	E	9.	B	9.	E
10.	A	10.	B	10.	C	10.	E
11.	C	11.	B	11.	C	11.	B
12.	C	12.	B	12.	C	12.	D
13.	D	13.	A	13.	B	13.	D
14.	E	14.	C	14.	B	14.	D
15.	D	15.	D	15.	B	15.	E
16.	A	16.	C	16.	D	16.	E
17.	D	17.	E	17.	E	17.	D
18.	D	18.	B	18.	D	18.	C
19.	A	19.	A	19.	C	19.	E
20.	D	20.	A	20.	C	20.	C
21.	E	21.	C	21.	A	21.	C
22.	A	22.	A	22.	A	22.	A
23.	B	23.	C	23.	D	23.	C
24.	E	24.	E	24.	D	24.	C
25.	B	25.	C	25.	D	25.	D
26.	D	26.	B	26.	E	26.	E
27.	D	27.	C	27.	E	27.	B
28.	C	28.	C	28.	E	28.	D
29.	A	29.	A	29.	A	29.	E
30.	E	30.	E	30.	A	30.	E
31.	D	31.	E	31.	C	31.	E
32.	B	32.	A	32.	D	32.	D
33.	D	33.	D	33.	C	33.	C
34.	A	34.	C	34.	D	34.	A
35.	E	35.	C	35.	D	35.	E
36.	D						
37.	E						
38.	E						
39.	C						
40.	A						
41.	D						
42.	D						
43.	B						
44.	E						
45.	C						

ABOUT THE AUTHOR

Cornelia Cocke has a BA from Dartmouth College and an MFA from Columbia University. She has taught for The Princeton Review since 1984.

The Princeton Review
Diagnostic Test Form ○ Side 1

1.

YOUR NAME: _____
(Print)   Last   First   M.I.

SIGNATURE: _____   DATE: ___ / ___ / ___

HOME ADDRESS: _____
(Print)   Number and Street

_____
City   State   Zip Code

PHONE NO.: _____
(Print)

IMPORTANT: Please fill in these boxes exactly as shown on the back cover of your test book.

2. TEST FORM

_____

3. TEST CODE

4. REGISTRATION NUMBER

5. YOUR NAME

First 4 letters of last name				FIRST INIT	MID INIT

6. DATE OF BIRTH

MONTH	DAY	YEAR
JAN		
FEB		
MAR		
APR		
MAY		
JUN		
JUL		
AUG		
SEP		
OCT		
NOV		
DEC		

7. SEX
- MALE
- FEMALE

SCANTRON® FORM NO. F-591-KIN
© SCANTRON CORPORATION 1989 3289-C553-5 4 3 2 1
ALL RIGHTS RESERVED.

Begin with number 1 for each new section of the test. Leave blank any extra answer spaces.

SECTION 1

1 A B C D E   26 A B C D E
2 A B C D E   27 A B C D E
3 A B C D E   28 A B C D E
4 A B C D E   29 A B C D E
5 A B C D E   30 A B C D E
6 A B C D E   31 A B C D E
7 A B C D E   32 A B C D E
8 A B C D E   33 A B C D E
9 A B C D E   34 A B C D E
10 A B C D E   35 A B C D E
11 A B C D E   36 A B C D E
12 A B C D E   37 A B C D E
13 A B C D E   38 A B C D E
14 A B C D E   39 A B C D E
15 A B C D E   40 A B C D E
16 A B C D E   41 A B C D E
17 A B C D E   42 A B C D E
18 A B C D E   43 A B C D E
19 A B C D E   44 A B C D E
20 A B C D E   45 A B C D E
21 A B C D E   46 A B C D E
22 A B C D E   47 A B C D E
23 A B C D E   48 A B C D E
24 A B C D E   49 A B C D E
25 A B C D E   50 A B C D E

SECTION 2

1 A B C D E   26 A B C D E
2 A B C D E   27 A B C D E
3 A B C D E   28 A B C D E
4 A B C D E   29 A B C D E
5 A B C D E   30 A B C D E
6 A B C D E   31 A B C D E
7 A B C D E   32 A B C D E
8 A B C D E   33 A B C D E
9 A B C D E   34 A B C D E
10 A B C D E   35 A B C D E
11 A B C D E   36 A B C D E
12 A B C D E   37 A B C D E
13 A B C D E   38 A B C D E
14 A B C D E   39 A B C D E
15 A B C D E   40 A B C D E
16 A B C D E   41 A B C D E
17 A B C D E   42 A B C D E
18 A B C D E   43 A B C D E
19 A B C D E   44 A B C D E
20 A B C D E   45 A B C D E
21 A B C D E   46 A B C D E
22 A B C D E   47 A B C D E
23 A B C D E   48 A B C D E
24 A B C D E   49 A B C D E
25 A B C D E   50 A B C D E

The Princeton Review
Diagnostic Test Form ○ Side 2

Completely darken bubbles with a No. 2 pencil. If you make a mistake, be sure to erase mark completely. Erase all stray marks.

Begin with number 1 for each new section of the test. Leave blank any extra answer spaces.

	SECTION 3	SECTION 4	SECTION 5	SECTION 6
1	A B C D E	A B C D E	A B C D E	A B C D E
2	A B C D E	A B C D E	A B C D E	A B C D E
3	A B C D E	A B C D E	A B C D E	A B C D E
4	A B C D E	A B C D E	A B C D E	A B C D E
5	A B C D E	A B C D E	A B C D E	A B C D E
6	A B C D E	A B C D E	A B C D E	A B C D E
7	A B C D E	A B C D E	A B C D E	A B C D E
8	A B C D E	A B C D E	A B C D E	A B C D E
9	A B C D E	A B C D E	A B C D E	A B C D E
10	A B C D E	A B C D E	A B C D E	A B C D E
11	A B C D E	A B C D E	A B C D E	A B C D E
12	A B C D E	A B C D E	A B C D E	A B C D E
13	A B C D E	A B C D E	A B C D E	A B C D E
14	A B C D E	A B C D E	A B C D E	A B C D E
15	A B C D E	A B C D E	A B C D E	A B C D E
16	A B C D E	A B C D E	A B C D E	A B C D E
17	A B C D E	A B C D E	A B C D E	A B C D E
18	A B C D E	A B C D E	A B C D E	A B C D E
19	A B C D E	A B C D E	A B C D E	A B C D E
20	A B C D E	A B C D E	A B C D E	A B C D E
21	A B C D E	A B C D E	A B C D E	A B C D E
22	A B C D E	A B C D E	A B C D E	A B C D E
23	A B C D E	A B C D E	A B C D E	A B C D E
24	A B C D E	A B C D E	A B C D E	A B C D E
25	A B C D E	A B C D E	A B C D E	A B C D E
26	A B C D E	A B C D E	A B C D E	A B C D E
27	A B C D E	A B C D E	A B C D E	A B C D E
28	A B C D E	A B C D E	A B C D E	A B C D E
29	A B C D E	A B C D E	A B C D E	A B C D E
30	A B C D E	A B C D E	A B C D E	A B C D E
31	A B C D E	A B C D E	A B C D E	A B C D E
32	A B C D E	A B C D E	A B C D E	A B C D E
33	A B C D E	A B C D E	A B C D E	A B C D E
34	A B C D E	A B C D E	A B C D E	A B C D E
35	A B C D E	A B C D E	A B C D E	A B C D E
36	A B C D E	A B C D E	A B C D E	A B C D E
37	A B C D E	A B C D E	A B C D E	A B C D E
38	A B C D E	A B C D E	A B C D E	A B C D E
39	A B C D E	A B C D E	A B C D E	A B C D E
40	A B C D E	A B C D E	A B C D E	A B C D E
41	A B C D E	A B C D E	A B C D E	A B C D E
42	A B C D E	A B C D E	A B C D E	A B C D E
43	A B C D E	A B C D E	A B C D E	A B C D E
44	A B C D E	A B C D E	A B C D E	A B C D E
45	A B C D E	A B C D E	A B C D E	A B C D E
46	A B C D E	A B C D E	A B C D E	A B C D E
47	A B C D E	A B C D E	A B C D E	A B C D E
48	A B C D E	A B C D E	A B C D E	A B C D E
49	A B C D E	A B C D E	A B C D E	A B C D E
50	A B C D E	A B C D E	A B C D E	A B C D E

FOR TPR USE ONLY	V1	V2	V3	V4	M1	M2	M3	M4	M5	M6	M7	M8

The Princeton Review
Diagnostic Test Form ○ Side 1

Completely darken bubbles with a No. 2 pencil. If you make a mistake, be sure to erase mark completely. Erase all stray marks.

1.

YOUR NAME: _____
(Print) Last   First   M.I.

SIGNATURE: _____ DATE: ___/___/___

HOME ADDRESS: _____
(Print)   Number and Street

_____
City   State   Zip Code

PHONE NO.: _____
(Print)

IMPORTANT: Please fill in these boxes exactly as shown on the back cover of your test book.

2. TEST FORM

3. TEST CODE

4. REGISTRATION NUMBER

5. YOUR NAME

First 4 letters of last name				FIRST INIT	MID INIT

6. DATE OF BIRTH

MONTH	DAY	YEAR
JAN		
FEB		
MAR		
APR		
MAY		
JUN		
JUL		
AUG		
SEP		
OCT		
NOV		
DEC		

7. SEX
- MALE
- FEMALE

⬦ **SCANTRON**® FORM NO. F-591-KIN
© SCANTRON CORPORATION 1989 3289-C553-5 4 3 2 1
ALL RIGHTS RESERVED.

Begin with number 1 for each new section of the test. Leave blank any extra answer spaces.

SECTION 1

1–50 A B C D E

SECTION 2

1–50 A B C D E

The Princeton Review
Diagnostic Test Form ○ Side 2

Completely darken bubbles with a No. 2 pencil. If you make a mistake, be sure to erase mark completely. Erase all stray marks.

Begin with number 1 for each new section of the test. Leave blank any extra answer spaces.

SECTION 3						SECTION 4						SECTION 5						SECTION 6					
1	A	B	C	D	E	1	A	B	C	D	E	1	A	B	C	D	E	1	A	B	C	D	E
2	A	B	C	D	E	2	A	B	C	D	E	2	A	B	C	D	E	2	A	B	C	D	E
3	A	B	C	D	E	3	A	B	C	D	E	3	A	B	C	D	E	3	A	B	C	D	E
4	A	B	C	D	E	4	A	B	C	D	E	4	A	B	C	D	E	4	A	B	C	D	E
5	A	B	C	D	E	5	A	B	C	D	E	5	A	B	C	D	E	5	A	B	C	D	E
6	A	B	C	D	E	6	A	B	C	D	E	6	A	B	C	D	E	6	A	B	C	D	E
7	A	B	C	D	E	7	A	B	C	D	E	7	A	B	C	D	E	7	A	B	C	D	E
8	A	B	C	D	E	8	A	B	C	D	E	8	A	B	C	D	E	8	A	B	C	D	E
9	A	B	C	D	E	9	A	B	C	D	E	9	A	B	C	D	E	9	A	B	C	D	E
10	A	B	C	D	E	10	A	B	C	D	E	10	A	B	C	D	E	10	A	B	C	D	E
11	A	B	C	D	E	11	A	B	C	D	E	11	A	B	C	D	E	11	A	B	C	D	E
12	A	B	C	D	E	12	A	B	C	D	E	12	A	B	C	D	E	12	A	B	C	D	E
13	A	B	C	D	E	13	A	B	C	D	E	13	A	B	C	D	E	13	A	B	C	D	E
14	A	B	C	D	E	14	A	B	C	D	E	14	A	B	C	D	E	14	A	B	C	D	E
15	A	B	C	D	E	15	A	B	C	D	E	15	A	B	C	D	E	15	A	B	C	D	E
16	A	B	C	D	E	16	A	B	C	D	E	16	A	B	C	D	E	16	A	B	C	D	E
17	A	B	C	D	E	17	A	B	C	D	E	17	A	B	C	D	E	17	A	B	C	D	E
18	A	B	C	D	E	18	A	B	C	D	E	18	A	B	C	D	E	18	A	B	C	D	E
19	A	B	C	D	E	19	A	B	C	D	E	19	A	B	C	D	E	19	A	B	C	D	E
20	A	B	C	D	E	20	A	B	C	D	E	20	A	B	C	D	E	20	A	B	C	D	E
21	A	B	C	D	E	21	A	B	C	D	E	21	A	B	C	D	E	21	A	B	C	D	E
22	A	B	C	D	E	22	A	B	C	D	E	22	A	B	C	D	E	22	A	B	C	D	E
23	A	B	C	D	E	23	A	B	C	D	E	23	A	B	C	D	E	23	A	B	C	D	E
24	A	B	C	D	E	24	A	B	C	D	E	24	A	B	C	D	E	24	A	B	C	D	E
25	A	B	C	D	E	25	A	B	C	D	E	25	A	B	C	D	E	25	A	B	C	D	E
26	A	B	C	D	E	26	A	B	C	D	E	26	A	B	C	D	E	26	A	B	C	D	E
27	A	B	C	D	E	27	A	B	C	D	E	27	A	B	C	D	E	27	A	B	C	D	E
28	A	B	C	D	E	28	A	B	C	D	E	28	A	B	C	D	E	28	A	B	C	D	E
29	A	B	C	D	E	29	A	B	C	D	E	29	A	B	C	D	E	29	A	B	C	D	E
30	A	B	C	D	E	30	A	B	C	D	E	30	A	B	C	D	E	30	A	B	C	D	E
31	A	B	C	D	E	31	A	B	C	D	E	31	A	B	C	D	E	31	A	B	C	D	E
32	A	B	C	D	E	32	A	B	C	D	E	32	A	B	C	D	E	32	A	B	C	D	E
33	A	B	C	D	E	33	A	B	C	D	E	33	A	B	C	D	E	33	A	B	C	D	E
34	A	B	C	D	E	34	A	B	C	D	E	34	A	B	C	D	E	34	A	B	C	D	E
35	A	B	C	D	E	35	A	B	C	D	E	35	A	B	C	D	E	35	A	B	C	D	E
36	A	B	C	D	E	36	A	B	C	D	E	36	A	B	C	D	E	36	A	B	C	D	E
37	A	B	C	D	E	37	A	B	C	D	E	37	A	B	C	D	E	37	A	B	C	D	E
38	A	B	C	D	E	38	A	B	C	D	E	38	A	B	C	D	E	38	A	B	C	D	E
39	A	B	C	D	E	39	A	B	C	D	E	39	A	B	C	D	E	39	A	B	C	D	E
40	A	B	C	D	E	40	A	B	C	D	E	40	A	B	C	D	E	40	A	B	C	D	E
41	A	B	C	D	E	41	A	B	C	D	E	41	A	B	C	D	E	41	A	B	C	D	E
42	A	B	C	D	E	42	A	B	C	D	E	42	A	B	C	D	E	42	A	B	C	D	E
43	A	B	C	D	E	43	A	B	C	D	E	43	A	B	C	D	E	43	A	B	C	D	E
44	A	B	C	D	E	44	A	B	C	D	E	44	A	B	C	D	E	44	A	B	C	D	E
45	A	B	C	D	E	45	A	B	C	D	E	45	A	B	C	D	E	45	A	B	C	D	E
46	A	B	C	D	E	46	A	B	C	D	E	46	A	B	C	D	E	46	A	B	C	D	E
47	A	B	C	D	E	47	A	B	C	D	E	47	A	B	C	D	E	47	A	B	C	D	E
48	A	B	C	D	E	48	A	B	C	D	E	48	A	B	C	D	E	48	A	B	C	D	E
49	A	B	C	D	E	49	A	B	C	D	E	49	A	B	C	D	E	49	A	B	C	D	E
50	A	B	C	D	E	50	A	B	C	D	E	50	A	B	C	D	E	50	A	B	C	D	E

FOR TPR USE ONLY	V1	V2	V3	V4	M1	M2	M3	M4	M5	M6	M7	M8

The Princeton Review
Diagnostic Test Form ○ Side 1

1.

YOUR NAME: _____
(Print)   Last   First   M.I.

SIGNATURE: _____ DATE: ___/___/___

HOME ADDRESS: _____
(Print)   Number and Street

_____
City   State   Zip Code

PHONE NO.: _____
(Print)

IMPORTANT: Please fill in these boxes exactly as shown on the back cover of your test book.

2. TEST FORM

_____

3. TEST CODE

4. REGISTRATION NUMBER

5. YOUR NAME

First 4 letters of last name				FIRST INIT	MID INIT

(A) through (Z) bubbles for each column

6. DATE OF BIRTH

MONTH	DAY	YEAR
○ JAN		
○ FEB		
○ MAR	(0) (0)	(0) (0)
○ APR	(1) (1)	(1) (1)
○ MAY	(2) (2)	(2) (2)
○ JUN	(3) (3)	(3) (3)
○ JUL	(4)	(4) (4)
○ AUG	(5)	(5) (5)
○ SEP	(6)	(6) (6)
○ OCT	(7)	(7) (7)
○ NOV	(8)	(8) (8)
○ DEC	(9)	(9) (9)

7. SEX

○ MALE
○ FEMALE

SCANTRON FORM NO. F-591-KIN
© SCANTRON CORPORATION 1989 3289-C553-5 4 3 2 1
ALL RIGHTS RESERVED.

Begin with number 1 for each new section of the test. Leave blank any extra answer spaces.

SECTION 1

1 (A) (B) (C) (D) (E)   26 (A) (B) (C) (D) (E)
2 (A) (B) (C) (D) (E)   27 (A) (B) (C) (D) (E)
3 (A) (B) (C) (D) (E)   28 (A) (B) (C) (D) (E)
4 (A) (B) (C) (D) (E)   29 (A) (B) (C) (D) (E)
5 (A) (B) (C) (D) (E)   30 (A) (B) (C) (D) (E)
6 (A) (B) (C) (D) (E)   31 (A) (B) (C) (D) (E)
7 (A) (B) (C) (D) (E)   32 (A) (B) (C) (D) (E)
8 (A) (B) (C) (D) (E)   33 (A) (B) (C) (D) (E)
9 (A) (B) (C) (D) (E)   34 (A) (B) (C) (D) (E)
10 (A) (B) (C) (D) (E)   35 (A) (B) (C) (D) (E)
11 (A) (B) (C) (D) (E)   36 (A) (B) (C) (D) (E)
12 (A) (B) (C) (D) (E)   37 (A) (B) (C) (D) (E)
13 (A) (B) (C) (D) (E)   38 (A) (B) (C) (D) (E)
14 (A) (B) (C) (D) (E)   39 (A) (B) (C) (D) (E)
15 (A) (B) (C) (D) (E)   40 (A) (B) (C) (D) (E)
16 (A) (B) (C) (D) (E)   41 (A) (B) (C) (D) (E)
17 (A) (B) (C) (D) (E)   42 (A) (B) (C) (D) (E)
18 (A) (B) (C) (D) (E)   43 (A) (B) (C) (D) (E)
19 (A) (B) (C) (D) (E)   44 (A) (B) (C) (D) (E)
20 (A) (B) (C) (D) (E)   45 (A) (B) (C) (D) (E)
21 (A) (B) (C) (D) (E)   46 (A) (B) (C) (D) (E)
22 (A) (B) (C) (D) (E)   47 (A) (B) (C) (D) (E)
23 (A) (B) (C) (D) (E)   48 (A) (B) (C) (D) (E)
24 (A) (B) (C) (D) (E)   49 (A) (B) (C) (D) (E)
25 (A) (B) (C) (D) (E)   50 (A) (B) (C) (D) (E)

SECTION 2

1 (A) (B) (C) (D) (E)   26 (A) (B) (C) (D) (E)
2 (A) (B) (C) (D) (E)   27 (A) (B) (C) (D) (E)
3 (A) (B) (C) (D) (E)   28 (A) (B) (C) (D) (E)
4 (A) (B) (C) (D) (E)   29 (A) (B) (C) (D) (E)
5 (A) (B) (C) (D) (E)   30 (A) (B) (C) (D) (E)
6 (A) (B) (C) (D) (E)   31 (A) (B) (C) (D) (E)
7 (A) (B) (C) (D) (E)   32 (A) (B) (C) (D) (E)
8 (A) (B) (C) (D) (E)   33 (A) (B) (C) (D) (E)
9 (A) (B) (C) (D) (E)   34 (A) (B) (C) (D) (E)
10 (A) (B) (C) (D) (E)   35 (A) (B) (C) (D) (E)
11 (A) (B) (C) (D) (E)   36 (A) (B) (C) (D) (E)
12 (A) (B) (C) (D) (E)   37 (A) (B) (C) (D) (E)
13 (A) (B) (C) (D) (E)   38 (A) (B) (C) (D) (E)
14 (A) (B) (C) (D) (E)   39 (A) (B) (C) (D) (E)
15 (A) (B) (C) (D) (E)   40 (A) (B) (C) (D) (E)
16 (A) (B) (C) (D) (E)   41 (A) (B) (C) (D) (E)
17 (A) (B) (C) (D) (E)   42 (A) (B) (C) (D) (E)
18 (A) (B) (C) (D) (E)   43 (A) (B) (C) (D) (E)
19 (A) (B) (C) (D) (E)   44 (A) (B) (C) (D) (E)
20 (A) (B) (C) (D) (E)   45 (A) (B) (C) (D) (E)
21 (A) (B) (C) (D) (E)   46 (A) (B) (C) (D) (E)
22 (A) (B) (C) (D) (E)   47 (A) (B) (C) (D) (E)
23 (A) (B) (C) (D) (E)   48 (A) (B) (C) (D) (E)
24 (A) (B) (C) (D) (E)   49 (A) (B) (C) (D) (E)
25 (A) (B) (C) (D) (E)   50 (A) (B) (C) (D) (E)

The Princeton Review
Diagnostic Test Form ○ Side 2

Completely darken bubbles with a No. 2 pencil. If you make a mistake, be sure to erase mark completely. Erase all stray marks.

Begin with number 1 for each new section of the test. Leave blank any extra answer spaces.

SECTION 3						SECTION 4						SECTION 5						SECTION 6					
1	A	B	C	D	E	1	A	B	C	D	E	1	A	B	C	D	E	1	A	B	C	D	E
2	A	B	C	D	E	2	A	B	C	D	E	2	A	B	C	D	E	2	A	B	C	D	E
3	A	B	C	D	E	3	A	B	C	D	E	3	A	B	C	D	E	3	A	B	C	D	E
4	A	B	C	D	E	4	A	B	C	D	E	4	A	B	C	D	E	4	A	B	C	D	E
5	A	B	C	D	E	5	A	B	C	D	E	5	A	B	C	D	E	5	A	B	C	D	E
6	A	B	C	D	E	6	A	B	C	D	E	6	A	B	C	D	E	6	A	B	C	D	E
7	A	B	C	D	E	7	A	B	C	D	E	7	A	B	C	D	E	7	A	B	C	D	E
8	A	B	C	D	E	8	A	B	C	D	E	8	A	B	C	D	E	8	A	B	C	D	E
9	A	B	C	D	E	9	A	B	C	D	E	9	A	B	C	D	E	9	A	B	C	D	E
10	A	B	C	D	E	10	A	B	C	D	E	10	A	B	C	D	E	10	A	B	C	D	E
11	A	B	C	D	E	11	A	B	C	D	E	11	A	B	C	D	E	11	A	B	C	D	E
12	A	B	C	D	E	12	A	B	C	D	E	12	A	B	C	D	E	12	A	B	C	D	E
13	A	B	C	D	E	13	A	B	C	D	E	13	A	B	C	D	E	13	A	B	C	D	E
14	A	B	C	D	E	14	A	B	C	D	E	14	A	B	C	D	E	14	A	B	C	D	E
15	A	B	C	D	E	15	A	B	C	D	E	15	A	B	C	D	E	15	A	B	C	D	E
16	A	B	C	D	E	16	A	B	C	D	E	16	A	B	C	D	E	16	A	B	C	D	E
17	A	B	C	D	E	17	A	B	C	D	E	17	A	B	C	D	E	17	A	B	C	D	E
18	A	B	C	D	E	18	A	B	C	D	E	18	A	B	C	D	E	18	A	B	C	D	E
19	A	B	C	D	E	19	A	B	C	D	E	19	A	B	C	D	E	19	A	B	C	D	E
20	A	B	C	D	E	20	A	B	C	D	E	20	A	B	C	D	E	20	A	B	C	D	E
21	A	B	C	D	E	21	A	B	C	D	E	21	A	B	C	D	E	21	A	B	C	D	E
22	A	B	C	D	E	22	A	B	C	D	E	22	A	B	C	D	E	22	A	B	C	D	E
23	A	B	C	D	E	23	A	B	C	D	E	23	A	B	C	D	E	23	A	B	C	D	E
24	A	B	C	D	E	24	A	B	C	D	E	24	A	B	C	D	E	24	A	B	C	D	E
25	A	B	C	D	E	25	A	B	C	D	E	25	A	B	C	D	E	25	A	B	C	D	E
26	A	B	C	D	E	26	A	B	C	D	E	26	A	B	C	D	E	26	A	B	C	D	E
27	A	B	C	D	E	27	A	B	C	D	E	27	A	B	C	D	E	27	A	B	C	D	E
28	A	B	C	D	E	28	A	B	C	D	E	28	A	B	C	D	E	28	A	B	C	D	E
29	A	B	C	D	E	29	A	B	C	D	E	29	A	B	C	D	E	29	A	B	C	D	E
30	A	B	C	D	E	30	A	B	C	D	E	30	A	B	C	D	E	30	A	B	C	D	E
31	A	B	C	D	E	31	A	B	C	D	E	31	A	B	C	D	E	31	A	B	C	D	E
32	A	B	C	D	E	32	A	B	C	D	E	32	A	B	C	D	E	32	A	B	C	D	E
33	A	B	C	D	E	33	A	B	C	D	E	33	A	B	C	D	E	33	A	B	C	D	E
34	A	B	C	D	E	34	A	B	C	D	E	34	A	B	C	D	E	34	A	B	C	D	E
35	A	B	C	D	E	35	A	B	C	D	E	35	A	B	C	D	E	35	A	B	C	D	E
36	A	B	C	D	E	36	A	B	C	D	E	36	A	B	C	D	E	36	A	B	C	D	E
37	A	B	C	D	E	37	A	B	C	D	E	37	A	B	C	D	E	37	A	B	C	D	E
38	A	B	C	D	E	38	A	B	C	D	E	38	A	B	C	D	E	38	A	B	C	D	E
39	A	B	C	D	E	39	A	B	C	D	E	39	A	B	C	D	E	39	A	B	C	D	E
40	A	B	C	D	E	40	A	B	C	D	E	40	A	B	C	D	E	40	A	B	C	D	E
41	A	B	C	D	E	41	A	B	C	D	E	41	A	B	C	D	E	41	A	B	C	D	E
42	A	B	C	D	E	42	A	B	C	D	E	42	A	B	C	D	E	42	A	B	C	D	E
43	A	B	C	D	E	43	A	B	C	D	E	43	A	B	C	D	E	43	A	B	C	D	E
44	A	B	C	D	E	44	A	B	C	D	E	44	A	B	C	D	E	44	A	B	C	D	E
45	A	B	C	D	E	45	A	B	C	D	E	45	A	B	C	D	E	45	A	B	C	D	E
46	A	B	C	D	E	46	A	B	C	D	E	46	A	B	C	D	E	46	A	B	C	D	E
47	A	B	C	D	E	47	A	B	C	D	E	47	A	B	C	D	E	47	A	B	C	D	E
48	A	B	C	D	E	48	A	B	C	D	E	48	A	B	C	D	E	48	A	B	C	D	E
49	A	B	C	D	E	49	A	B	C	D	E	49	A	B	C	D	E	49	A	B	C	D	E
50	A	B	C	D	E	50	A	B	C	D	E	50	A	B	C	D	E	50	A	B	C	D	E

FOR TPR USE ONLY	V1	V2	V3	V4	M1	M2	M3	M4	M5	M6	M7	M8